FATHER IN THE KITCHEN

FATHER IN THE KITCHEN

Bruce Beeby

Illustrations by
INGRID JOHNSON

MICHAEL JOSEPH : LONDON

First published in Great Britain by
Michael Joseph Limited
52 Bedford Square
London W.C.1
1977

ISBN 0 7181 1543 0

Phototypeset in Great Britain by
Western Printing Services Limited, Bristol
and printed and bound by
Billing & Sons Limited, Guildford,
London and Worcester

To my wife and family who have gallantly sampled all kinds of experiments without complaint.

CONTENTS

INTENTION

This is not a specialist cook book. It contains recipes from Italy, Germany, Wales, Russia, China, England, Australia, etc. I had intended to include one from Patagonia but that turned out a failure. It is designed specifically:

1. To get Father into the kitchen.

2. To encourage his flair and imagination.

3. To suggest recipes which will encourage any cook to get the best out of the materials they intend to use. None of those meat and two veg jobs.

4. To interest Mother as well. She should find stimulating ways of cooking ordinary meals economically and well. Many recipes which require expensive ingredients and involved methods of cooking have been omitted: i.e., Coq Au Vin cooked to perfection in a £4 bottle of Chambertin. Fathers will instead use their very best bottle of Spanish or Yugloslavian plonk.

5. To provide a wide variety of recipes suitable for most occasions.

6. To get Father to cook the Christmas feast – the final triumph! The perfect stuffing for his Christmas masterpiece will be found on page 107.

This Father has cooked the Christmas dinner for twenty-seven years. He has been married for twenty-eight and it is rumoured that he missed the seventeenth year because he was discovered sozzled under the Christmas tree at 8.30 in the morning. Since it appears that he suffered a temporary blackout, there is little he can say in his defence. Mother had to take over and the turkey stuffing was excellent as always. Hence, she should be allowed to *borrow* the book.

CHAPTER 1

Epistles

EPISTLE TO MOTHER

Dear Mother,

You've bought this book, so with a bit of luck you may get Father into the kitchen. I should point out that according to the dictionary the meaning of 'luck' is good or bad fortune. How you interpret it depends on what happens there. It is a certainty that you will be left with a mountain of washing up, burned pots and pans, the floor to be scrubbed, and the condition of the stove — indescribable! You will also consider that you could have prepared the meal better, quicker and more efficiently yourself.

That seems to cover any possible bad fortune. Now think of the good fortune. Think of the fun you might have missed: think of the joy on Father's face when you praise him for his first cooking of excellent soggy rice, for the painstaking care taken in the preparation of his lumpy Béchamel sauce, for the tenderness of his charred roast. Be an optimist. He will improve in time and your foresight will be rewarded. After all, who is going to look after you and the kids (if any) should you break a leg, get run over by a bus, or suffer some other minor disaster. Be charitable. With a gentle smile, help him make a roux, or a beurre manié, or a lumpless Béchamel sauce. Flatter him. Keep him happy. Keep his glass filled — but not too often. You don't want the roast to slide on to your best table-cloth as he attempts to carve it.

Even suffer the insufferable when he's confident that he's finally cooked the perfect meal and mutters, 'Everybody knows that men are the best cooks. They have so much imagination.' Just do the washing up as quietly as possible and write a letter to women's lib.

There is another way of using this book. Ban him from the kitchen and use it yourself. Allow him in to do the washing up.

EPISTLE TO FATHER

Dear Father,

Mother has had her little note, so why not you? I had intended to leave out specific measurements except where they seemed essential, but the editress has decreed otherwise, saying that I ought to help the poor inexperienced male a little more. I considered this a good enough reason to start 'Men's Lib' but she smiled at me and I succumbed. Well – partially.

As I don't want to burden you with metric weights and measurements, you will find that quantities indicated are in tablespoonfuls and cupfuls of this and that – or in pinches of, or a dash of, etc. – although meat quantities are generally given in pounds. You'll find a metric table, an oven temperature chart, and a glossary of terms which may be unfamiliar to you at the end of chapter 2.

But be warned. Measurements and oven temperatures should not be followed slavishly. The villainous cook is one who sticks rigidly to weights and measurements, to scales and thermometers. One can't give an exact recipe. Think of the imponderables. How good is the meat, how fresh, how tough, how old? Do you want it rare or well done? How good is your stove? Are your vegetables diced or cut in chunks? Are they fresh or deep frozen? And well, I mean to say, how much is a tablespoon of butter? One book says $\frac{1}{2}$ oz, another $\frac{3}{4}$ oz. Confusion is rampant. And a tablespoon of flour? Should it be rounded, level, or heaped? Same with liquid measurements: 1 cup is on average $\frac{1}{2}$ pint. If you're using a cup as big as a shaving mug – be careful. And how long should you cook your offering? On what heat? If I find a recipe which says to cook at Gas Mark 6, I cook on Gas Mark 8; if it says 2, I cook on 4; if it suggests 9, I despair. The moral of the above is that I have a lousy stove.

So be flexible. Interpret all the cooking instructions with intelligence and commonsense. As for cooking time, do you want your lamb cooked for 8 minutes per lb as I read in one famous French cook book, or 15–20 minutes which I read in another? It's up to you. If your roux is crumbly add more butter or fat; if too greasy add more flour. If your sauce is too thick add more liquid; if too thin make a beurre manié and thicken with that. If the vegetables are too salty rinse in masses of water and re-heat. If still too salty rinse in masses of water and re-heat. If still too salty – eat them and suffer. In other words, always season carefully. You can always add, but it's not so easy to subtract, especially if you are preparing a sauce which has to be reduced. If the meat is burned to a cinder chuck it out or feed it to a not too fussy cat and take the family out to dinner. An expensive alternative, but never mind, you'll do better next time.

Now tomatoes: everywhere you will read 'skin them and de-seed them'. I never bother. If you do, what have you got left? A bit of pulp. Have you considered the price of tomatoes? Aunt Agatha may complain that they are indigestible but there's a simple answer to that. Don't invite her to dinner when using fresh tomatoes.

And when you come to consume your labour of love, make the family discuss it. Drag out a complaint if it's really terrible. And if it's a howling success, it's nice to be appreciated. Mind you, there is a penalty to pay. You'll have to make a song and dance about your wife's successes. And why not? The preparation of a good meal should be a pleasure because you want to please those you care about. You may now reach for your handkerchief and dry your eyes.

Don't be afraid of simplicity. Try to preserve the essential flavour of whatever you are trying to cook. Don't suffocate it in left-over gravy or an indifferently made, incompatible sauce; or smother it with grated cheese browned under the grill – as so often happens. We men must strike. Down with the mystique of cooking. To the fore with commonsense, care, flair, imagination and personal taste.

General Notes on Imagination, Improvisation and Substitution

You could be familiar with much of the following. Never mind. Read on: you may come across something unexpected.

Quantities given are for four people unless stated otherwise.

A Good Cook

Apart from the professionals who cook for money (and they're not always good) the best cooks are those who get pleasure out of cooking for guests and family. Don't forget the basic ingredients however: care, attention and quite often a bit of extra trouble. A superb meal doesn't happen by accident.

Batter

If you're wondering why it always falls off when you come to deep fry, it's because whatever you are trying to cook was wet when you applied the batter. So dry well first.

If you are deep frying, don't put all your battered pieces into a frying basket and then lower it into your boiling fat. The batter will stick to the basket and, particularly in the case of fish, break up when you come to move it. Instead, lower your empty basket into the fat and add gently, one by one, each piece to be fried. Use a straining spoon to avoid blistered fingers.

Béchamel Sauce

There is absolutely no excuse for a lumpy Béchamel sauce (see page 121). I've never known this method to fail.

Butter

For butter, you can read margarine, or oil and butter, or just oil, or clarified fat. Avoid the latter unless it is for a meaty stew or the frying of an egg.

Cloves

Some people can't stomach them; they remind them of the dentist's chair. But don't leave them out. Used with discretion, they provide an excellent and unusual flavour. Essential for the fish chowder on page 65.

Cooking Oils etc

For oil, read groundnut oil, coconut oil, or vegetable oil. Don't use that expensive olive oil for cooking unless you are very rich. Treasure it and use it for salads. When buying olive oil make sure that it is a reputable brand. Olive oil can be as variable as Spanish plonk.

Cream

For cream, read double cream; if double cream is unavailable try single cream; if no single cream, try bottle-top cream; and if still without cream reduce a quantity of milk to half its volume. It is wise to have a stand-by tin of imitation cream, but remember not to let it boil. (It is not as good of course, but useful if the little woman hasn't done the shopping properly). You will find a few recipes which state double cream. In these cases, only double cream will do.

Fat

It can be spooned off but there's always some left. Get rid of this by letting the fat rise to the surface of your liquid then draw an absorbent paper kitchen towel over it. If it's a fatty piece of meat or poultry taking time to cook, pour off most of the liquid into a bowl and place in the fridge while cooking continues. If given enough time, the fat will rise to the top and harden, the stock will sink to the bottom. You can then return these precious meat juices to the pan or use them another day. Don't worry, even if put in the fridge while still very hot, the bowl won't burst. And I put mine in the freezing compartment! The fridge still works after years of this abuse.

Garlic

For garlic, read more garlic, less garlic, or no garlic. Depends on who's coming to dinner. Mind you, the last instruction is a little ridiculous if you intend to cook the excellent Chicken with Twenty Cloves of Garlic given on page 100.

Garnish

Don't forget to garnish – almost everything. Attractive-looking food is palatable. Accept gracefully the 'oo's and ahhh's' that will greet the presentation of your artistically decorated meal.

Don't take so long over it that food meant to be hot is cold by the time it reaches the dining-room table. Use sliced or quartered tomatoes, sliced hard-boiled eggs, anchovy fillets, shredded celery (leaves and all), the ubiquitous parsley in sprigs or finely chopped, watercress, green and black olives, thinly sliced green and red peppers, baby gherkins, a sprinkling of paprika, etc. In fact, use almost anything which *you* think is compatible with the meal you have prepared.

Ham

When you're out of ham and you want ham, boil a few rashers of bacon. It's ham, of a sort!

Herbs

Unless you grow them yourself, you'll have to put up with the dried varieties in bottle. Buy small quantities. Keep them well sealed when not in use. Many of them work well: dried mint for example. Pour a little boiling water over them before using; it helps to bring out the flavour. Don't buy dried chives. You might just as well use a pinch of sawdust. The same applies to dried parsley. Try to buy herbs of French origin. They are stronger, and generally last longer, so use with caution.

When you haven't got the prescribed herb, use your imagination and substitute. Bay leaves, so necessary in nearly all casseroles and stews, don't keep long. However, if you are a really sneaky person, many shops around London have bay trees growing outside their premises. Most people don't recognise their potential so they remain inviolate. Regent Street is a good hunting ground. Enough said.

Hot Spices and Condiments

The use of these is very much a matter of personal taste. If you like hot curry and chilli dishes, as I do, use more than the prescribed amount.

Ingredients

Many recipes are by-passed because some of the ingredients are not always to hand or are hard to get. Substitute, with imagination and audacity. It's known as the trial-and-error method, to be practised when you are friendless and guests are not expected. Let the family suffer first. If they complain, belt 'em. After all, who's the biggest?

Lettuce

Most cook books suggest that you tear a lettuce apart when preparing a salad rather than by cutting. This is not because you haven't got a decent sharp knife. It's simply that if you cut it, the vitamin C is lost more quickly.

Liver

Pour boiling water over it before you start to cook. This seals, tenderises, and preserves the nutritional value.

Meat

When considering the economy of the household, be sure to read the recipes relating to grilled or fried steak and the suggested substitutes. (See pages 75–7.)

And if you're thinking of fillets of veal, hesitate. You'll need an overdraft. Buy instead a leg of veal, and cut out the fillets yourself. (See page 90.) Where do you think the butcher gets his fillets? A whole leg of veal will cost not much more (even less perhaps) than 1 lb of the supposed real thing. When you've cut out the fillets, put them between two pieces of greaseproof paper and bash them flat with the rolling pin or a bottle or, if you have a well-equipped kitchen, with a cutlet bat. You now have escalopes of veal and a lot of good meat still on the bone. If you are careful you shouldn't mess up the leg too much. If you do, strip the bone and make a stew or veal paprika, etc. Two excellent meals for the price of one. What could be better? Finally, this is one of the best occasions when it is worthwhile simmering the bone. You should get a good veal jelly out of it. (Throw in a pig's trotter as well.) The dog can then have the bone when you've finished with it.

That's enough about meat for the moment otherwise you'll never get to the succulent recipes. You'll find further comments about meat at the beginning of the meat section.

Mushrooms

The number of mushrooms indicated in many recipes refer to the commercially produced button mushrooms. If you're lucky enough to come across the flat, field kind, buy an equal quantity of those instead. Eight button mushrooms might equal three field mushrooms. Never, never, never use tinned mushrooms. If you do, you've wasted your money.

Optional

Quite often something is suggested as optional. This doesn't mean that leaving the ingredient out is a good thing. It's simply that some of the items may be expensive or difficult to get. In which case, omit and still have a bash at the recipe.

Oven Temperatures

Oven temperatures throughout the book are described as very low, low and slow, medium, moderate, moderately hot, hot, and hot as —. There is a table at the end of this chapter which will make them clear to you. Settings and temperatures are given for both electric and gas stoves.

Paprika

For paprika, always read Hungarian paprika. I find most other kinds tasteless and bland. If you have to use other brands pep them up by the addition of a pinch or two of cayenne pepper.

Parsley

Most of the goodness is in the stalks. Use the leaves for garnish, and flavour with the stalks.

Peanuts

Peanuts are an excellent substitute for the more expensive nuts. They can be used in salads, with French beans, cream cheese etc.

Pork

The weekend joint is pork and somebody has forgotten to buy apple purée or cooking apples. Do not despair. Look in the cupboard: you're certain to find some redcurrant jelly there. Use it now, mixed with a good dollop of French mustard, and the day is saved.

Pottery

Pottery plates and serving dishes are a boon. You can shove them in the oven any old time and they won't crack provided they aren't exposed to a direct heat. Hot plates are very essential for good cooking. They can be put under the grill with a low heat. It is worth buying a few, particularly serving dishes, then you won't have to balance delicate china on the top or side of the stove – crash! – or in too hot an oven – crack! They look nice too.

Prawns

The prawns we have to buy these days are generally peeled and deep frozen; and I'm suspicious of those offered as fresh peeled prawns. They were probably deep frozen and defrosted before being put on display. The quality is invariably poor except for those which have come from the coldest of seas. The colder the water in which they once lived, the better the flavour. Try, therefore, to buy the prawns labelled North Atlantic prawns. Avoid the cocktail prawns unless you like cotton wool.

Seasoning

For seasoning, read salt and freshly ground black pepper. Quantities to taste. Usually less pepper than salt. If you haven't got a pepper mill, go out and buy one; the bottles of coarsely ground pepper now available, providing you replace the lid after using, are a satisfactory substitute. If you're making a white sauce and you're fussy about its colour use white pepper. I wouldn't.

Sour Cream

For sour cream (if you haven't got any) read cream or bottle-top cream to which you've added a good squirt of lemon and/or a drop or two of white vinegar. Let it stand for an hour or two before using. Or try a mixture of yoghurt and cream. It's less rich and more astringent than the real thing. I personally prefer this mixture unless you want a very creamy dish and it is particularly suitable for a stroganoff or goulash. Quite often plain yoghurt will suffice and it is much cheaper.

Spices

Try warming them a little until a few of them pop. It brings out their full flavour. Then crush in a pestle and mortar.

Stock

For stock – if you haven't got a stock pot, and not many of us do have these days – make it from one of the excellent stock cubes on the market, dissolved in an appropriate amount of water. Stick to chicken and beef cubes. You might even be lucky enough to come across a fish stock cube in Soho's Brewer Street.

You can simmer those left-over turkey, duck, or chicken bones. I've simmered them for hours supported by the addition of herbs and vegetables of various kinds, but one does tend to finish up with an enormous gas bill and a pallid liquid tasting of herbs and vegetables of various kinds. The best way to produce a stock of any strength is to reduce it considerably.

If you boil the herbs and vegetables with an added stock cube, you can produce a reasonable stock and a reduced gas bill.

Tomatoes

Try to buy Moroccan tomatoes, or any imported from a hot sunny climate. Or button-sized ones before they have grown into tasteless, watery, uniform round red eggs. It is the sun which creates flavour. Why people continue to persist in buying the commercial tomato is something I don't understand. So never pass a greengrocer selling higgledy-piggledy ones. These comments, of course, don't apply during winter. We have to put up with what is offered then. For tomato sauce, I prefer to use a tin of Italian tomatoes, heated up with a little sugar and mushed up. Much more flavour and infinitely cheaper.

Tomato Purée and Tomato Paste

Tomato paste is salted. Tomato purée is unsalted. Do not confuse either with sauce from a bottle now widely known as tomato ketchup. This is well-seasoned.

Vegetables — Deep Frozen

Ignore the packet instructions. Simply drop them in a pot with a little water and a good knob of butter. Cover and shake the pot frequently to stop burning. The ice, as it melts, will provide extra liquid. Uncover and boil away any excess liquid when nearly cooked. Better than swamping in a pot of salted water.

Wine

For white wine you can nearly always substitute a dry cider; on occasions use demi-sec if your wife fancies finishing off the bottle; or lemon juice and stock; or if really desperate, one or two tablespoons of wine vinegar mixed with about a pint of stock. A slightly sweet wine is usually better than a dry one.

While on the subject of wine, do you, when dining out, go through that rigmarole of tasting it, of pursing your lips appreciatively as if you'd just had a suck of a lemon, of then nodding your head approvingly and accepting the proffered bottle with a gracious smile? How often have you had the courage and – dare I say it – the knowledge to send it back? My procedure is to wave an airy, knowledgeable hand and invite the wine waiter to fill the glass. If it's no good I can still send it back. It will probably end up in the Coq au Vin that I'm about to order.

Which brings me to the sneaky point of this note. Father, when cooking with wine, should always have a little taste. He can then nod his head approvingly if he likes. He can even mutter 'Hmm, yes. Much too good,' to the steaming stove. If his 'Hmm, yes' is *very* appreciative, I can see no reason why he shouldn't drink it all. It would, however, be uncharitable not to offer a glass to Mother. He now has two alternatives. He can send out for a bottle of plonk or change the menu. Instead of Beef Casserole in Red Wine, he could produce Beef Casserole 'Au Naturel'.

OVEN TEMPERATURES

Electric oven settings F	As described in this book	Gas oven marks
200–250	Very low	$\frac{1}{4}$–1
300–325	Low or slow	2–3
350–375	Medium or moderate	4–5
400–425	Moderately hot	6–7
450–475	Hot to very hot	8–9
500	Don't burn the food!	

MEASUREMENTS

Tablespoon	— rounded, unless otherwise indicated
Dessertspoon	— rounded, unless otherwise indicated
Teaspoon	— rounded, unless otherwise indicated
Cupful	— means $\frac{1}{2}$ pint
Wineglass	— 4 oz glass

GLOSSARY OF TERMS AS UNDERSTOOD BY FATHER

Al dente
Soft on the outside, resistant to the teeth inside. Used in relation to rice, pasta and dried vegetables.

Beurre manié
Butter and flour mixed together in equal parts for the purpose of thickening. Best used by dropping a knob at a time into a proposed gravy or sauce.

Blanch
Strictly speaking to make white, bleach; to wrinkle the skins on almonds so that the skin peels off by dropping into boiling water. Father drops things into hot water for about 1 minute because it seems to work. That's what it means here, anyway.

Bouquet garni
The classic combination is a bayleaf, thyme, and parsley tied together or parcelled in a piece of muslin. Father might try other herbs but he should never omit a bayleaf.

Clarified fat
Melt the fat with a little water and let it boil furiously for a minute. Pour in bowl, and when a little cooler place in fridge to let it harden. The impurities will sink to the bottom with the water, and you can carefully take the purified fat off the top.

Clarified butter
Melt the butter. Spoon off froth on top. Don't let it brown. Then strain through muslin. Store in fridge. Very useful when cooking fish or veal. If you're really enthusiastic, put the strained butter into a piece of muslin and squeeze out excess moisture, then store.

Court bouillon
Used to poach fish. A simple bouillon is made by simmering a roughly chopped carrot and onion, a bouquet garni and $\frac{1}{4}$ cup wine vinegar in 4 cups water. But there are variations which you must choose for yourself. Use some white wine (or even red for something like mackerel) and stock instead of water and drop in a dozen whole peppercorns. Strain before or after use. Better before if there is any danger of breaking up the fish. Can be reduced and used to flavour a sauce.

Meat glaze
That's what Father calls the delicious stuff in the bottom of the pan which comes out of the joint, and after the excess fat has been removed. Strictly speaking, it is the concentrated juice extracted from meat. If you want to make some, boil a bit of old beef with a pig's trotter or veal bone, together with a bouquet garni and a few chopped vegetables. Don't salt. Strain, and reduce until it is nice and gluey. The jelly from the trotter or veal bone should help to achieve this. Use to flavour sauces and gravy. That is meat glaze of a sort.

Par-boil
Half-cook.

Roux
Made by sprinkling flour into butter, oil or fat to make a thick paste. Liquid is then added and stirred until it thickens smoothly.

Sauté

From the French verb 'sauter' meaning to jump. When potatoes are sautéed, they jump around in the pan as they cook – or they should, providing the cook gives the handle of the pan a good wiggle from time to time. In other words, when you want to sauté something, make sure it keeps moving during cooking.

CHAPTER 3

Preludes and Fugues

(Hors d'oeuvre and salads)

Hors d'oeuvre are a leisurely and practical way of taking the edge off a ravenous appetite before settling down to a magnificent main course. They also have the advantage of allowing the cook to disappear from the table from time to time to deal with an unexpected little difficulty like opening a tin of potatoes to replace burned ones, to put out the fire because the fat has caught light, or to rescue a curdling sauce which shouldn't have been left anyway. The guests will munch and chat on contentedly. In such emergencies a willing helper will keep all glasses well topped-up.

Unfortunately nowadays, cubes of cheese, salted peanuts, crisps, cheese straws, pickled onions (their hearts pierced by little plastic daggers) are passed off as hors d'oeuvre. This won't do. They're only a nibble and an unfitting prelude to your perfectly balanced meal. You can get that lot at a decent pub any Sunday morning for the price of a pint.

You'll find something more interesting overleaf. Try the spicy prawn or chicken starters, peaches and crab if you've just had a large increase in salary, or the attractive petalled tomato and hard-boiled egg.

Many of the salads, their flavours overlapping and intermingling as in all good fugues, can be served 'on the side' with the masterpiece. Those marked with * are a meal in themselves.

FRENCH BEANS AND PRAWNS

1 pkt (12 oz) frozen whole beans, 3 tablespoons oil, 1 tablespoon lemon juice, a pinch of cayenne pepper, a pinch paprika, seasoning, $\frac{1}{2}$ lb peeled prawns, 2 hard-boiled eggs.

Cook the beans as described in notes on frozen vegetables. While still warm add a mixture of oil, lemon juice, cayenne pepper, paprika and seasoning. Chill. Add the prawns when they have defrosted. Do it carefully so that the beans are not broken up. Garnish with slices of hard-boiled eggs and the other half of the lemon cut into wedges.

HARICOT OR BUTTER BEAN SALAD

It seems a pity that haricot and butter beans are not used more widely. They're excellent vegetables. Perhaps the following will tempt you.

1$\frac{1}{2}$ cups of haricot or butter beans, 1 level tablespoon salt, 2 cloves of crushed garlic, 2 tablespoons vinegar.

If using haricot beans, cover with plenty of water and soak overnight with the other ingredients added. If using butter beans, they cook quite quickly if only soaked for about an hour. Cook either kind of bean in the marinade until nutty. Don't overcook. Haricot beans may need to be simmered for two hours; butter beans can be cooked in as little as forty minutes. Strain.

Two extensions:

1.   With Salami

4–6 tablespoons vinaigrette dressing, 1 finely chopped onion, 2 crushed cloves of garlic, 4 tablespoons roughly chopped garlic-flavoured salami sausage, parsley.

Pour the vinaigrette dressing over the beans while they are still warm. Add the other ingredients and serve when the salad is properly cold. Garnish.

2.   With Chicory and Anchovies

4–6 tablespoons vinaigrette dressing, 2 crushed cloves of garlic, 3 heads of chicory, 1 tin chopped anchovy fillets.

Add the dressing as above. When cold mix in the chicory roughly chopped and most of the anchovy fillets. Keep three or four whole for garnishing.

NOTE: Because the anchovies tend to be salty, either soak them in milk first, or use only $\frac{1}{2}$ tablespoon of salt in the marinade for the beans.

BEEF ROLLS WITH FRANKFURT SALAD AND PINEAPPLE SLAW*

To be prepared in four parts.

1.   Beef Rolls

8 thin slices of cold roast beef or corned beef (the tinned kind will not do), 1 tablespoon finely chopped green pepper, $\frac{3}{4}$ cup cottage cheese.

Mix the green pepper with the cottage cheese and spread some of it on to each piece of beef. Roll and skewer with a toothpick.
NOTE: You can use horseradish sauce instead of the cheese, but the cheese-pepper filling is more unusual.

2.   The Frankfurt Salad

$\frac{1}{2}$ cup sliced frankfurts, $1\frac{1}{2}$ cups of diced cooked potatoes, $1\frac{1}{2}$ cups of thickly grated carrots, $\frac{1}{4}$ cup mayonnaise, 2 tablespoons finely chopped parsley, seasoning.

Mix them all together.

3.   The Pineapple Slaw

2 cups shredded cabbage lightly blanched, $\frac{3}{4}$ cup diced eating apple, $\frac{1}{2}$ cup cubed pineapple (if not using fresh pineapple a small tin, drained of its juice, will do), $\frac{1}{4}$ cup diced celery, $\frac{1}{4}$ cup mayonnaise, $\frac{1}{4}$ cup chopped walnuts, seasoning.

Mix that lot together, except for the walnuts. Do not peel the apple.

4.   Curry Sauce

$\frac{3}{4}$ teaspoon paprika, $\frac{1}{2}$ teaspoon curry powder, $\frac{3}{4}$ cup oil, $\frac{3}{4}$ cup wine vinegar, 1 teaspoon dry mustard, 1 teaspoon sugar, seasoning.

Mix the curry powder and the paprika together first in a little of the oil. Then add the rest of the ingredients with the remaining oil. Beat until very well mixed. Chill.

TO ASSEMBLE: You will need a good lettuce. Separate leaves and place two cup-shaped ones on each plate. Fill one cup with the frankfurt mixture and the second one with the slaw. Sprinkle the walnuts over the slaw. Place two beef rolls on each plate. Serve with the curry sauce.

It is better if all the ingredients have been well chilled before assembly. Sounds a lot of trouble but well worth it. It is a magnificent looking salad and ideal for a hot summer's day. You can put each section into plastic containers and take on a picnic.

CELERY, OLIVE AND WALNUT SALAD

1 stick celery, 6 stoned and chopped green olives, ½ cup chopped walnuts, 2 tablespoons double cream, 2 tablespoons mayonnaise, salt, watercress.

Chop the celery into pieces about two inches long. Arrange in a small circular bowl as if building a stockade. Mix the other ingredients together with additional bits of finely chopped celery, but omit the watercress and a few walnuts which will be used for garnishing. Add salt to taste. Pour the mixture into the centre of the bowl, then garnish.

CHICKEN LIVER STARTER (HOT)

1 lb chicken livers, 2 slices ham, 2 tablespoons butter, flour, lemon juice, croûtons, seasoning, oil, parsley.

Chop up the chicken livers and the ham. Sauté very gently in butter. Season. Sprinkle lightly with flour, stir liver in pan, add stock and a squirt or two of lemon juice. Cover pan and simmer very gently for about ten minutes. For the croûtons you can use either French bread or ordinary white bread. Remove the crusts and shape into pieces about two inches square. Allow two pieces for each person. Cover a pan with a liberal amount of oil and drop the bread in. Brown over a moderate heat otherwise the croûtons will blacken. On both sides of course. Most of the oil will be absorbed by the bread. If the oil completely vanishes add a little more.

Pour the livers and a little of the sauce over the croûtons and serve garnished with chopped parsley.

CURRIED CHICKEN AND MELON SALAD*

Should be enough for six. You will notice that I suggest that the melon should be diced as neatly as possible, but if you have a ball cutter, use that to scoop out the fruit. It won't make it taste any better but presentation will be much more attractive.

2 cups diced, cooked chicken, ½ cup mayonnaise, ½ tablespoon finely chopped onion, ¾ cup chopped celery, 6 tablespoons lemon juice, 1 tablespoon curry powder (or to taste), 3 tablespoons sour cream, 1 medium-sized melon (honeydew or canteloupe), 3 tablespoons oil, salt to taste.

Mix the diced chicken with the mayonnaise, onion, celery, 2 tablespoons of the lemon juice and salt to taste. Mix the curry powder into the sour cream, and when smooth combine with the chicken mixture. Chill. Halve the melon, remove the seeds, then scoop out the flesh in fairly large dice, almost down to the rind. Marinate in the remaining lemon juice mixed with the oil and season lightly.

Chill the shells.

Finally, mix the melon cubes or balls into the chicken–curry mixture, being careful not to mash up the melon. Scoop the lot into the shells and return to fridge until everything is chilled right through.

Offer chopped cashew nuts, chutneys, and dried coconut as accompaniments.

CHICKEN AND RICE BUFFET*

This is one of those cold, help-yourself dishes, ideal for a party as it can be prepared well in advance. I prepared it for my daughter's wedding party and she's still speaking to me. You should be able to feed six with this little lot.

1 3–3½ lb chicken, 1 onion, bouquet garni, 1½ cups long grain rice, 3 tablespoons Worcestershire sauce, 1 cup double cream, 2 tablespoons tomato purée, ½ cup mayonnaise, 2 teaspoons lemon juice, 1 cup cooked peas, 6 stoned olives, 1 red pepper, 3 tablespoons vinaigrette, seasoning.

You can buy jointed chicken pieces, otherwise do it yourself, and place in the pot with a roughly chopped-up onion, the bouquet garni and seasoning. Cover with water and simmer until cooked. (You can use boiling chicken which will also give you a decent stock for a future soup.) Roasting chicken pieces should only take about 45 minutes, boiling chicken might take a couple of hours depending on how old it is.

When cooked, drain and cool. Remove the flesh from the bones. Cut into convenient-sized pieces. A convenient size is a question of how many mouths you are going to feed and how big those mouths are.

Meanwhile cook the rice in salted water until cooked, but not overcooked – about 15 minutes. Drain and cool. Make a sauce by mixing together the Worcestershire sauce, cream, tomato purée, mayonnaise and the lemon juice. Add seasoning if necessary. Stir in the chicken pieces.

Assemble as follows: Mix into the rice the cooked peas, half the olives which you should chop, and most of the pepper cut into strips. Stir in the vinaigrette dressing. Spread this rice mixture on a large platter. Pour the chicken mixture into the centre of the dish and garnish with the remaining olives (halved) and slivers of red pepper.

CHILLED CUCUMBER AND SOUR CREAM

One of the most refreshing salads imaginable. A marvellous contrast to nearly all main dishes.

1 cucumber, 3 tablespoons sour cream, chopped mint and/or dried dill, paprika, salt.

Slice the cucumber and arrange so that each slice overlaps. Sprinkle with salt. Spread the sour cream over the top. Sprinkle with mint or dried dill or a mixture of both. Place in fridge and chill until very cold. Don't get it so cold that the cucumber becomes transparent and loses its flavour. Just before serving sprinkle with a little paprika. If you put the paprika on the cucumber before chilling it will become gluggy.

NOTE: A mixture of sour cream and yoghurt – or simply just yoghurt – is equally satisfactory. It's a matter of preference: Father thinks yoghurt is a good idea – and it's cheaper.

CUCUMBER ROUNDS

1 cucumber, 2 tomatoes, mayonnaise, seasoning, ½ green or red pepper.

Cut the cucumber into rounds about two inches long. Scoop out the pulp. Mash up and mix with 2 chopped tomatoes, a little mayonnaise, seasoning to taste, and finely chopped pepper. Stuff this mixture back into the cucumber rounds and chill.

You can add all kinds of things to this filling. Finely chopped chicken, ham, tiny bits of left-over potato, a sprinkling of mint, etc.

Garnish before serving.

STUFFED EGGS

Nothing remarkable about a stuffed egg but some of the fillings might stir your imagination. A very pleasant and comparatively easy hors d'oeuvre to prepare.

Eggs (as many as you need), mayonnaise, seasoning, condiments of all kinds, a drop or two of bottle-top cream.

Hard boil the eggs, shell, halve, and remove the yolks without damaging the white casing. Mash yolk and mix in one or more of the following, plus a little of what you fancy.

1. Curry powder
2. A drop of mayonnaise
3. A drop of bottle-top cream
4. Paprika and/or cayenne pepper
5. Nutmeg
6. A drop of Worcestershire sauce
7. Mashed capers
8. Finely diced gherkins

Don't let the egg yolks get too moist. Go easy on the liquid additions.

Stuff the mixture back into the white halves and present garnished with crisp celery sticks.

My favourite is a mixture of curry powder, a drop of mayonnaise, and a taste of cayenne pepper added to the mashed egg yolks.

FATHER'S DIFFERENT SALADS

Father, fed up with eternal tomato or green salads, has let his imagination run riot and come up with the following:

1. Cottage Cheese Mix-up

One of his most enterprising and delicious efforts. No quantities are given. Balance to your own taste; you can't go wrong.

Cottage cheese, torn lettuce, spring onions, chopped or sliced green pepper, chunks of unpeeled red apple, raisins, equal parts honey and lemon for a dressing.

Mix all together.

2. Watercress and Mandarin Mix-up

1 bunch watercress, 3 seedless mandarins or tangerines, 2 tablespoons oil, 1 tablespoon wine vinegar, 1 teaspoon lemon juice, 1 teaspoon honey.

Make the dressing and add to mixed-up watercress and mandarins. That's only a little nibble for four so increase quantities proportionately if you think you'd like it.

3. Celery and Beetroot Mix-up

Anybody could have thought this one up. But it is uncommon. And pleasant.

Chop up some celery and mix with equal chunks of beetroot. Toss in a vinaigrette dressing. Over to you for quantities used.

HAM AND SLAW SALAD*

1 small white cabbage, 1 hard-boiled egg, $\frac{3}{4}$ cup of mayonnaise, $\frac{1}{2}$ cup white seedless grapes, cayenne pepper, seasoning, $\frac{1}{4}-\frac{1}{2}$ cup chopped or flaked almonds, slices of ham for four, 1 cup cubed fresh pineapple.

Shred the cabbage after removing the hard centre. Mash the hard-boiled egg (you could use two eggs if you like) and mix into the mayonnaise. Add the grapes, a pinch of cayenne pepper and very little salt and black pepper, and finally the shredded cabbage and almonds. Serve with slices of ham and the pineapple pieces (I wouldn't use tinned pineapple for this recipe). Simple and refreshing. Peanuts instead of almonds are an excellent substitute.

MANDARIN SALAD

Unusual.

1 tin mandarins (or fresh peeled ones if available), $1\frac{1}{2}$ cups cream cheese, 2 tablespoons raisins, 1 lettuce heart, a few radishes, watercress.

If using tinned mandarins, drain the juice. Pile the cheese onto a plate, sprinkle with the raisins, surround with mandarin pieces, torn lettuce leaves and a few radishes. Garnish with watercress. You could mix some of the raisins into the cheese, using the remainder for garnish.
Serve with French bread.

MIXED SALAD*

This is often known as a Russian salad.

3 cups diced cooked potatoes, 2 cups cooked chopped chicken (or chopped cold meat of almost any kind or a mixture of whatever you have left over), 1 cup cooked peas, 3 chopped sticks celery, ½ cup cooked diced beetroot, 2 diced cooking apples, 3 or 4 hard-boiled eggs, a few gherkins, 1 cup mayonnaise.

Mix all the ingredients together in a salad bowl. You can vary the quantities to suit yourself. Almost anything goes. Serve, if you like, with slices of garlic sausage if short of cooked meat.

PEACHES AND CRAB

6 fresh peaches, 1 cup crab meat, ½ cup double cream, salt and paprika.

Cut the top of each peach, scoop out the stone and some of the flesh. Mix the flesh with the crab meat, the cream, a little bit of salt and paprika. Stuff the peaches with this mixture. Chill and serve cold. Don't forget to sprinkle each peach with a little more paprika just before serving. (Enough for six.)

POTATO SALAD WITH BLACK OLIVES

You don't like black olives? Keep on trying; they are an acquired taste.

6 black olives, 3 anchovy fillets, 1 large red or green pepper, 2 tomatoes, 2 tablespoons double cream, ½ cup mayonnaise, 3 cups diced cooked potatoes, seasoning.

Stone the olives, chop up the anchovy fillets, slice the pepper thinly, chop up the tomatoes. Add the cream to the mayonnaise. Mix all these together with the potato, except for the olives and a few strips of the pepper. Season, but careful with the salt because of the anchovies. Put in a salad bowl and garnish with the olives and the strips of pepper. Or you can chop the olives and mix them into the salad. I suggested them as a garnish so that the uninitiated can avoid them.

SPICY PRAWN STARTER

For a dinner party, enough for four.

4 tablespoons butter, 2 tablespoons flour, ¾ cup milk, ¾ cup cream, 2 tablespoons tomato purée, 1 tablespoon Worcestershire sauce, cayenne pepper, salt, 1 cup sliced mushrooms, 1 lb peeled prawns, lemon juice, breadcrumbs.

Melt butter, add flour and make a roux. Don't let it darken. Stir in the milk and cream (milk first) slowly. Simmer for five minutes. Add tomato purée, Worcestershire sauce, a good pinch cayenne pepper, and salt to taste.

Sauté the mushrooms separately in butter. Add to the sauce, together with the prawns. Add the juice of ½ lemon. Pour into a buttered casserole or into individual heat-proof dishes. Sprinkle with breadcrumbs. Dot with butter and bake in a moderate oven for 20 minutes. Brown under the grill if necessary.

CURRY AND RICE SALAD*

¾ cup long grain rice, 1½ cups diced cooked meat of any kind, ½ cup sultanas, ½ cup mayonnaise, 1 tablespoon oil, 1 onion, 1 clove of garlic, 1½ tablespoons curry powder (variable according to strength and personal taste), 1 tablespoon flour, ¾ cup water or stock, seasoning, 1 cucumber, 4 tomatoes, 1 lettuce heart, 1 lemon.

Cook rice in salted water until al dente. Mix the meat, rice, sultanas and mayonnaise together. Chop up the onion and sauté with a crushed clove of garlic in the oil. Add the curry powder and the flour mixed together. Cook for a couple of minutes over a low heat. Then add about ¾ cup of water or stock, stirring all the time. Season sauce to taste. Then stir into the meat and rice and let it stand for several hours.

Slice the cucumber thinly and soak in vinegar until ready to serve. Quarter the tomatoes and season. Separate the lettuce leaves, arrange in cups on serving plate, and fill each cup with the curry mixture. Garnish with lemon chunks and serve with the cucumber and tomatoes.

PETALLED TOMATO SALAD WITH HARD-BOILED EGGS

Très artistic. Prepared in a moment.

Large tomatoes, seasoning, sugar, hard-boiled eggs, mayonnaise.

Slice the tomatoes but not right through. Season. Sprinkle with a little sugar. Let the sugar dissolve and then insert a slice of hard-boiled egg into each pocket. Drop a dollop of thick mayonnaise onto each tomato rose. I said, très artistic. Garnish.

STUFFED TOMATOES

These can be a bit of trouble, but well worth it if carefully prepared. The stuffings are infinite. An hors d'oeuvre where Father can use his renowned 'flair and imagination'.

The initial preparation is basic: Cut the top off each tomato, large ones if you can get them. Scoop out most of the flesh without damaging the casing. Sprinkle the inside of each case with salt, turn them upside down and let them drain. You will be able to use some of the flesh with the stuffing, and the surplus can be used to flavour casseroles and stews or to make home-made tomato sauce.

Suggested Hot Stuffings

1. Mash some hard-boiled eggs and mix with a little creamy Béchamel sauce. Sprinkle with grated cheese. Extra salt is probably unnecessary because of the salt content of the cheese. Bake in a medium oven for not more than ten minutes or the sides of the tomato will collapse. This applies to all the hot dishes. Brown the cheese under the grill.

2. Mix chopped chicken with a little very thick sauce made with a roux and some reduced strongly flavoured chicken stock. Season to taste. The addition of a few finely chopped almonds ensures an interesting texture.

3. Sauté a finely chopped onion and chopped mushrooms in butter. Mix with a little of the tomato flesh. If too wet, place in a saucepan and

evaporate the excess liquid by fast boiling. Season to taste. Make plenty of stuffing so that the tomatoes, when filled, have a domed appearance. Sprinkle each tomato with breadcrumbs. Cover loosely with foil and bake in moderate oven.

4. Mix together a little cooked patna rice, a finely chopped blanched onion, chopped parsley, a few flaked almonds pounded in a pestle and mortar, a finely chopped cooked chicken liver, or tiny bits of cooked chicken, nutmeg, a few raisins, and a drop or two of thick chicken sauce. Season to taste. Bake in moderate oven.

This mixture with one or two additions makes an excellent and unusual stuffing for chickens (see page 97).

5. One part white breadcrumbs soaked in stock or milk, squeezed as dry as possible and mixed with two parts of finely chopped poultry, ham or pork. Sauté a finely chopped onion until translucent with a little garlic, then add to the meat and breadcrumbs together with a sprinkling of mild herbs like parsley or chives. Season. Bind with the yolk of an egg. Sprinkle lightly with a few breadcrumbs or grated cheese. Don't cover with foil. Bake in moderate oven.

Suggested Cold Stuffings

1. Use the pulp and mix with a good strong horseradish sauce.

2. Mix left-over flaked fish with mayonnaise. You could use a drained tin of tuna or salmon.

3. Fill the cases with cream cheese. Garnish with nuts. You could also mix a few seedless raisins into the cheese.

4. Mix cream cheese with stoned dates.

Most of the above mixtures can be varied to suit your own taste, and some of the hot ones served cold instead. If cold, offer them as an hors d'oeuvre, if hot as an accompaniment to the main meal or as a separate course.

TOMATO SALAD

A lovely salad if presented attractively, which Father will always do. Slice the tomatoes carefully, arrange them neatly on a flat serving plate, sprinkle with sugar, season, and pour over a vinaigrette dressing. Sometimes you can add finely chopped onion; almost always use a modicum of finely chopped garlic. Finally, garnish with chopped parsley or a sprinkling of chopped fresh chives.

Never make a combined lettuce and tomato salad because they are basically incompatible. If you want to offer both, serve them separately.

Why include such a simple recipe? It's because of the terrible things people do with it. They sometimes spoon the tomatoes and the vinaigrette dressing onto the meat plates so that the astringent vinegar and oil runs into the delicate wine sauce you have prepared with such loving care. You can overcome this by insisting that each guest and each member of the family has a side plate. This applies to all salads containing a dressing: side plates always.

TUNA COLESLAW*

2 tins tuna to ½ white cabbage, 1 tin anchovy fillets, 3 chopped celery sticks, 1 or 2 sliced red and/or green peppers, 2 chopped peeled oranges, vinaigrette dressing, 2 tablespoons fresh mint (or mint flakes first soaked in a little boiling water), seasoning.

Cut out the hard stalk and shred the cabbage finely. Chop the anchovies into small bits reserving two or three for garnishing. Mix all the ingredients together and finally add as much vinaigrette dressing as you feel is necessary. Season, but careful with the salt because of the anchovies. Garnish with the anchovy fillets cut in halves.

OR

Instead of the vinaigrette dressing, mix 3 tablespoons of double cream (whipped) with the same amount of mayonnaise. If you haven't any cream handy, double the amount of mayonnaise.

TUNA SALAD*

1 tin tuna, 2 hard-boiled eggs, 3 tablespoons oil, 1 tablespoon lemon juice, 1 lb cooked diced potatoes, 2 finely chopped onions, 3 roughly chopped tomatoes, seasoning.

Roughly chop the eggs, make a dressing of the oil and lemon juice, and mix in with all the other ingredients. Season.

OR

You can use mayonnaise as above and omit the oil and lemon dressing.

CHAPTER 4

Unmurdered Vegetables

Is there a reek of boiling cabbage or cauliflower coming from your kitchen? If so, you have committed murder.

One of the commonest faults in British cooking is that so many vegetables are boiled to death. They arrive at the table mushy, having lost their shape and resilience. *Never overcook,* and re-read my note about the cooking of frozen vegetables on page 23. Cooked to perfection with 'flair and imagination', many vegetables can be served as a separate course.

AUBERGINES

Not to everybody's taste. Usual method of cooking is to slice the unpeeled aubergine into slanting $\frac{1}{4}''$-wide pieces. Salt and leave to drain for about an hour, then fry in a liberal amount of oil until light brown on both sides. Aubergines are invariably used in ratatouille and moussaka, see pages 55 and 81. However, they are becoming much more popular and are a change from the more conventional vegetables.

AUBERGINES WITH SAVOURY STUFFING

2–4 aubergines, salt and freshly ground pepper, 6–10 stoned and chopped black olives, 2–3 tablespoons breadcrumbs, chopped parsley, 12 mashed capers, 2–4 finely chopped anchovy fillets, $\frac{1}{4}$ teaspoon origano or marjoram.

Cut the unpeeled aubergines in half. Scoop out some of the flesh. Salt the halves and leave to drain for an hour. Make a stuffing of the other ingredients including the pulp. The quantities can be adjusted to suit the size of the aubergines and personal taste. Half a teaspoon of anchovy sauce can be used instead of the more expensive fillets, but go easy on the salt. Perhaps a little black pepper. Put back this stuffing loosely into the aubergines, and liberally anoint each half with oil. Place in an oven pan, smeared with oil, which can be covered. Bake slowly in a medium oven for thirty minutes.

AUBERGINES WITH MEAT STUFFING

2–4 aubergines, 1 onion, 1 clove of garlic, $\frac{1}{2}$ cup minced or chopped meat, 3 tablespoons grated cheese, 1 small tin tomatoes, 1 teaspoon anchovy sauce, seasoning.

Prepare the aubergines as above, only take out more of the pulp. Chop the onion and garlic very finely. Mix into the meat (it can be any kind of cooked meat including bits of chopped ham) with half the cheese, the aubergine pulp, the tomatoes, the anchovy sauce, and cook until the cheese melts and the liquid has almost completely evaporated. Check seasoning. Place some of this mixture into each of the aubergine 'boats'. Sprinkle with the remaining cheese and bake in a medium oven in a heat-proof pan smeared with oil for thirty minutes. Brown under the grill if necessary.

AUBERGINES, TOMATOES AND ONION

2–4 aubergines, 1 finely chopped onion, 1 crushed clove garlic, seasoning, 2–3 tomatoes, chopped parsley.

Cut the aubergines in half, sprinkle with salt and place them, cut side down, in a pan containing a little warm oil and cook slowly until tender. Remove from the pan and scoop out most of the flesh. In the same pan sauté the chopped onion with the garlic. Add a drop more oil if necessary. When the onion softens, take out of the pan, mix with the aubergine pulp, season, and put back into the aubergine halves.

Slice the tomatoes until you have enough to completely cover the top of each half of aubergine. Season very lightly and bake in a medium oven for thirty minutes or until the tomatoes begin to soften. Garnish with a liberal amount of chopped parsley.

BEANS: FRENCH AND RUNNER

Usually boiled in salted water until tender. Father's methods will always be to use whole or halved French beans rather than those cut on the slant à la Mrs Beeton. If fresh beans, cook conventionally. If frozen, cook as described on page 23.

FRENCH BEANS AND ALMONDS

1 lb whole beans, butter, 1 tablespoon flaked almonds.

Cook the beans. Melt 1 tablespoon butter and lightly brown the flaked almonds. Mix them and any of the butter not absorbed into the beans.

FRENCH BEANS AND ONIONS

1 lb whole beans, 1 onion, butter.

Cook the beans, then strain. Chop the onion and sauté lightly in a little butter. Add the whole beans. Turn up the heat so that the onion and the beans start to brown.

RUNNER BEANS AND TOMATOES

You can use runner beans or French beans. If using the runner beans, don't wait until they are a foot long. Pick or buy them when young, top and tail and string if necessary.

1 lb beans, 3 tomatoes, oil, 1 clove garlic, seasoning.

Half cook the beans in salted water. Chop up the tomatoes and cook them in a little oil together with a crushed clove of garlic. Add the beans and continue to cook until they are tender. Check seasoning.

TINNED FRENCH BEANS

You want beans and you haven't got them, so keep a tin of whole French beans in the cupboard. They're not the best, but something can be done with them in an emergency.

1 large tin French beans, 2 rashers bacon, 3 tablespoons butter, 1–2 cloves finely chopped garlic, 1 tablespoon chopped parsley.

Drain the liquid from the tin of beans and rinse thoroughly. Dice the bacon. Melt the butter. Sauté the bacon in the butter over a gentle heat until it is nearly cooked. Add the beans, turn up the heat, and fry until the beans start to go brown and the bacon to crisp. During this process turn the beans carefully so as not to break them up. Season. Place in a serving dish and mix in the finely chopped garlic. Garnish with parsley.

BEANS AND CHEESE

French beans, grated cheese, butter, seasoning.

Cook and drain the beans, sprinkle with cheese, dot with butter and brown under the grill. Don't oversalt the beans when cooking them because of the salt in the cheese.

BEANS AND PEARS

3 rashers bacon, 1 cup stock, 3 peeled pears, 1 lb whole frozen French beans, seasoning, parsley.

Cut the bacon into thin strips. Sauté gently in oil. Add, after five minutes, the stock, the pears peeled, cored and chopped. Simmer for ten minutes. Then add the whole French beans and continue to simmer until cooked. Spoon off most of the excess liquid. Season with salt and plenty of freshly ground black pepper. Sprinkle with parsley.

BEANS: BROAD

I hated broad beans when I was a kid. Maybe you did too. With advancing years I have acquired a soupçon of wisdom and they have been revalued. Now I find them a versatile vegetable.

BROAD BEAN MIX-UP

1 lb fresh or frozen broad beans, 6 mushrooms.
All or some of the following: carrots, peas, French beans, 1 inch long pieces of celery, sweet corn.
1–3 tablespoons butter depending on quantities used, Béchamel sauce, seasoning.
*(*OPTIONAL*: grated cheese and breadcrumbs.)*

If using frozen broad beans, cook as suggested on page 23. Use the same method for any other frozen vegetables which you may be using. They can all be put in the pot together.

Lightly sauté the mushrooms.

If using fresh vegetables, such as carrot and celery, dice the carrot and cut the celery as indicated, and cook separately in a pan with a little butter and 1–2 tablespoons water. Shake the pan or stir occasionally to ensure that they don't brown. Not more than five minutes: Don't overcook. They should still be firm when added to the broad beans. Celery, particularly, is nicer if undercooked. Then add the mushrooms.

Make a Béchamel sauce; how much depends on the quantity of vegetables used. If there is any liquid left over when the vegetables have finished cooking (there should be very little), it can be added to the white sauce for extra flavour. Finally mix in all the vegetables, garnish and serve. Remember that this dish is a Broad Bean mix-up and broad beans should predominate.

OPTIONAL ALTERNATIVE: sprinkle vegetables and sauce with grated cheese and breadcrumbs. Brown under the grill.

BROAD BEANS AND PORK

1 lb broad beans, 2 slices belly pork, 1 tablespoon oil, 1 chopped onion, seasoning.

Cook the beans. Chop up the pork into small cubes. Smear the pan with oil and fry the onion and the pork very slowly for at least thirty minutes. Cover the pan if possible. If you prefer to have the onions and pork lightly browned, do so by turning up the heat towards the end of cooking. Mix into the drained beans, season to taste, and serve.

BROAD BEANS AND YOGHURT

1 lb broad beans, 1 crushed clove garlic, 4–5 tablespoons yoghurt, a beurre manié (page 25), seasoning, parsley.

Cook the beans. Mix the garlic into the yoghurt. Heat and thicken slightly with the beurre manié. Pour over the drained beans, check seasoning, garnish with parsley and serve.

BRUSSELS SPROUTS

A brussel is a brussel is a brussel. It is one of the most murdered of vegetables, so often served as a mushy slop.

Cook them in salted water but do not overcook them. They should still be firm when you drain them. Then chop them roughly and throw into a pan with a liberal quantity of butter. The heat should be low, and the brussels should absorb as much butter as possible. Season to taste and finally add whatever fresh cream you can spare.

OR

Cook them as above and throw them whole into a frying pan containing very hot butter. Swirl them around until they are browned all over.

CABBAGE

Murder! Another cabbage has been done over. Close the windows. Poor old cabbage: it's top of the list, you'll find, when making a study of vegetable homicide. The method of extermination is simple. Cut a lovely fresh cabbage into two or three pieces and shove in a pot. Cover with salted water and slowly boil it to death, then throw the poor dripping corpse into a serving bowl.

Those not guilty should skip the next para. The guilty ones read on.

First, shred the cabbage as you would for slaw. Place in a wide-bottomed saucepan with a little water, salt, and 2 tablespoons of butter. Cover and simmer gently until slightly softened, and that's all. The cabbage is cooked, and no revolting aroma has engulfed the neighbours.

It can be an excellent accompaniment for many meats but is best of all with some kind of Polish ring sausages or frankfurts (see page 113). And beef in cabbage leaves is a magnificent meal (see page 82).

CARROTS

I'm sure every self-respecting cook is familiar with the following methods or something similar, but just in case:

GLAZED CARROTS

Cut into rounds and place in a pot with a little butter, a drop of water, and 1 teaspoon of sugar. Season lightly and cover the pan. Simmer until cooked shaking the pan from time to time. If necessary add a little more water. The liquid left in the pan should be syrupy. Before serving, stir in some chopped mint.

CARROTS AND ONION

Sauté one finely chopped onion in butter. Add a drop of water and the carrots cut into rounds. Season and proceed as above. When tender, add a little bottle-top cream to the tiny bit of liquid remaining. Sprinkle with chopped parsley.

CAULIFLOWER

You can cut off the green bits; I don't, I chop them up and use them as well. Boil in a little salted water and serve. Or cook and cover with a Béchamel sauce, grated cheese, and brown under the grill. Or add a lot of cheese to the Béchamel sauce and it becomes a cheese sauce.

Here are some different methods.

HONEY CAULIFLOWER

1 cauliflower, butter, 1 tablespoon thin honey, seasoning, 1 tablespoon grated cheese.

Par-boil the cauliflower. Butter an oven-proof dish. Pull the cauliflower apart and place the flowerets in the dish. Dribble a little honey over each piece, season and sprinkle with cheese. Place in a medium oven until the cheese melts (about 10 mins).

GARLIC FRIED CAULIFLOWER

1 cauliflower, oil, 1–2 cloves garlic, seasoning.

Par-boil the cauliflower. Break it up. Lightly cover a frying pan with oil – not too much. Toss in the pieces of cauliflower and crushed garlic cloves. Season. Turn up the heat and mash up the cauliflower with a fork, turning it over and over until it is well browned.

CAULIFLOWER AND HERBS

1 cauliflower, butter, lemon juice, herbs such as chives, chervil and parsley.

Par-boil the cauliflower. Break up the flowerets and sauté in butter and a sprinkling of lemon juice. Add a pinch or two of the suggested herbs with seasoning to taste.

CELERY

CELERY COOKED IN THE OVEN

Another victim of the salt and boiling water method: try cooking it in the oven instead.

1 good bunch of celery, 3 tablespoons butter, meat juices or good stock, seasoning.

Cut the celery sticks into pieces about 5–6 inches long. Place in an oven-proof dish which can be covered. Add the butter and a drop of water or stock. Season. I intentionally overdo the black pepper. Pepper and celery seem to love one another. Try it once, you might like it. If you have any good meat juice, add it. Or if you are cooking a roast at the same time, you can sneak some from the roasting pan. If you use a strong stock made from a stock cube, go easy on the salt. The cubes can be very salty.

Cover the celery with loose foil, then the lid and place in the oven. You can cook it on the bottom of the oven if you are cooking a roast at the same time and cooking time will be about two hours. If not, place on the centre shelf in a moderately hot oven when the cooking time will be about $1-1\frac{1}{4}$ hours. Check from time to time to see that there is always a little liquid left in the bottom of the dish. You can thicken this slightly with a beurre manié if you like.

COURGETTES

A delicious vegetable which is now readily available. Very versatile. Never peel them; if you have to, you've been robbed. You've been sold a marrow instead and a marrow *isn't* a big courgette although they belong to the same family.

COURGETTE ROUNDS

The basic method of cooking them is simple and very good. Slice into rounds and fry gently in butter until tender and lightly browned. Season.

(OPTIONAL: squirt with a drop of lemon.)

COURGETTE CHIPS

This may seem rather unenterprising but Father knows best. Delicious cooked this way.

Slice the courgettes into little thin chips about half the size of the conventional potato chip. Salt them and let drain for an hour. Pat dry with Mother's clean new tea towel if she isn't looking – otherwise, pat them dry as best you can. (Don't use your scruffy handkerchief.) Dip each chip in flour and deep fry until brown and crisp.

COURGETTES AND CHEESE

1 lb courgettes, 1 egg, 4 tablespoons cream, 2 tablespoons grated cheese, butter, seasoning.

Half cook the courgettes, sliced into rounds, in salted water. Drain and put in a buttered oven dish. Beat the egg and mix it with the cream and half the grated cheese. Pour this mixture over the courgettes, season, sprinkle with the remainder of the cheese, dot with butter and bake in a hot oven until the cheese browns.

COURGETTES AND TOMATOES

1 lb courgettes, $\frac{3}{4}$ lb tomatoes, butter, seasoning.

Slice the courgettes in rounds. Salt and let them drain for an hour. Chop up the tomatoes. When ready to cook, place both vegetables in a wide-bottomed saucepan with a liberal amount of butter. Season. Cook on a low heat until the courgettes are tender.

COURGETTES, NUTS AND SULTANAS

1 lb courgettes, 1 clove garlic, 1 tablespoon wine vinegar, 1 teaspoon sugar, $\frac{1}{2}$ teaspoon anchovy sauce, 2 tablespoons pine kernels or chopped almonds, chopped parsley, 2 tablespoons sultanas, seasoning.

Slice the courgettes into rounds. Lightly sauté the garlic in a little oil. Add the courgettes and brown on both sides. Then mix the vinegar and the sugar in 1 tablespoon of warm water; add the anchovy sauce, the pine kernels (better than chopped almonds), a little chopped parsley, the sultanas and pour over the courgettes. Season to taste. Mix well without damaging the courgette rounds.

If you would prefer more of the sweet-sour sauce, increase the quantities of the vinegar, water, and sugar.

CUCUMBER
COOKED CUCUMBER

1 cucumber, seasoning, $\frac{1}{2}$ cup cheese sauce, more grated cheese, butter.

Cut the cucumber into chunky pieces. Boil in salted water. They should come out of the pot still reasonably firm. Drain, season and cover with a thick cheesy sauce. (That's a Béchamel sauce with a lot of cheese – see page 121.) Sprinkle with the extra cheese, dot with butter and brown under the grill.

LETTUCE
LETTUCE STEWED

Included for those Fathers who have grown their own and would like to use them up before they bolt.

Wash the lettuces well, remove outer leaves, stew until tender in a little salted water. Drain well. Squeeze out excess moisture. Chop roughly. Melt 1 tablespoon of butter and add the juice of 1 lemon before it starts to brown. Return the lettuce to the pan and mix with the lemon butter sauce which should accommodate three reasonably sized lettuces. Season, but not much pepper.

LEEKS
A POOR MAN'S ASPARAGUS

Leeks, seasoning, ½ cup thick cheese sauce, grated cheese, butter.

Buy enough leeks to feed four. Cut off the tops and the very bottom of the white part. Split down the middle, but not all the way down so the leeks flower out. It makes washing easier. They can be very gritty so rinse carefully, separating the leaves as much as possible without pulling them apart. Rather than go through this palaver, I am inclined to buy leeks from supermarkets as they have been trimmed and washed effectively. Boil in salted water until tender, but do not overcook. Place in a heat-proof dish, season, and cover with a thick cheese sauce – i.e., Béchamel sauce with as much cheese melted in it as you like. Sprinkle with grated cheese, dot with butter and brown under the grill.

LEEKS AND TOMATOES

Leeks, oil, seasoning, cayenne pepper, 2 tomatoes, 2–3 chopped cloves of garlic, chopped parsley, lemon juice.

Enough leeks for four prepared as described in preceding recipe. Having prepared them, warm 2–4 tablespoons oil in a frying pan. Then snuggle the leeks side by side. Season: not too much black pepper – sprinkle instead with a good pinch of cayenne pepper. Cook over a moderate heat, turning each leek carefully until browned all over. When tender, remove, place in a serving dish and keep warm.

Chop the tomatoes and throw them into the pan from which you have taken the leeks together with the garlic and a handful of chopped parsley. Turn up the heat and cook for 3–4 minutes. The tomatoes should remain a little firm. Pour over the leeks, squirt the lot with lemon and serve.

A marvellous flavour, and a chance to present vegetables simply cooked.

MUSHROOMS

We all know how to cook mushrooms. But do we all know how to get the best out of them? Father offers four recipes which should please, even if you are familiar with them.

MUSHROOMS AND POTATOES

A fact, often overlooked, is that potatoes and mushrooms are very, very 'sympatico'.

1 lb potatoes, ¾ lb mushrooms, 1 onion, parsley, ¼ lb cheese, 1–2 cloves of garlic, butter, seasoning, ¼ teaspoon nutmeg, 1 small carton of cream.

Slice the peeled potatoes and the mushrooms. Chop up the onion, chop up quite a lot of parsley – stalks and all, grate the cheese (Emmenthal or Gruyère are best but 'rat trap' is still excellent) and chop the garlic into the tiniest pieces. Grease a gratin dish with butter and place in it first a layer of sliced potatoes and then one of sliced mushrooms. Sprinkle with a little onion, a touch of garlic, some of the parsley and finally a portion of grated cheese. Season each layer with very little salt, freshly ground pepper and a few grains of nutmeg. Repeat until all the ingredients have been used, reserving some of the cheese for a final topping.

Heat the cream (single cream or bottle-top cream) with 1 table-spoon of water. Pour this over the mixture. Sprinkle with the remainder of the cheese. Dot with butter. Bake in a medium oven on the centre shelf for an hour. If you intend it to accompany an oven-prepared dish, it can be cooked on the bottom shelf, at the same time. In this case, allow at least $1\frac{1}{2}$ hours. It's a difficult dish to spoil and the oven temperature at which it is cooked is not vital. The slower the oven, the longer the cooking.

MUSHROOMS, MINT AND GARLIC

$\frac{3}{4}$ lb mushrooms, 1 crushed clove of garlic, 2–3 tablespoons oil, 1 tablespoon chopped mint, seasoning.

Slice the mushrooms, stalks and all. Mix the garlic into the oil. Add the chopped mint. Place the mushrooms into a pot and pour the mixture over them. Cover the pot, season and stew gently until cooked. The quantities are up to you and variable. The main consideration is how much you like garlic.

MUSHROOMS AND PARMESAN CHEESE – BAKED

$\frac{3}{4}$ lb large flat mushrooms, 2 tablespoons chopped ham or crisply fried bacon, chopped parsley, Parmesan cheese, seasoning, $\frac{1}{4}$ glass white wine (optional), oil.

Remove the stalks from the mushrooms and place the caps, top side down, in an oven-proof dish smeared with oil. Chop the stalks finely. Mix with the chopped ham, parsley, and about 1 tablespoon of Parmesan. Add the white wine at this stage if you are going to use it. Spoon some of the mixture onto each mushroom cap. Anoint each cap and its filling with oil. Cover with foil and bake in a moderate oven for thirty minutes. Add extra oil if necessary to keep the mushrooms moist.

Very little seasoning is needed – the merest sprinkling on the mushroom caps before adding the chopped mixture.

MUSHROOMS GRILLED

A much better way of cooking them, in my opinion, than sautéing in butter or oil, especially if you are lucky enough to buy field mush-rooms and not the commercial variety. Remove stalks and season lightly. Fill the cups with oil and place under hot grill. Keep moist by adding more oil: don't let them dry out.

MUSHROOM LOAF

1 lb mushrooms, 2 tomatoes, 1 onion, 2 tablespoons butter, $\frac{1}{4}-\frac{1}{2}$ cup mixed chopped nuts, 1 cup fresh breadcrumbs, 1 egg, seasoning.

Slice the mushrooms and chop up the tomatoes and onion. Melt the butter and simmer the onion for a few minutes. Mix with all the other ingredients. Season. You may need a second egg for binding. Shape into a loaf and place on a greased baking dish. Brush with extra melted butter and bake in the oven till brown, should take about thirty minutes in a medium hot oven. It can be cooked in a small rectangular cake tin.

ONIONS

FRIED

They are usually chopped, seasoned, chucked into a frying pan with a little oil until well browned, and are often rather greasy. If Spanish onions are available, the following method is excellent and the onions will be crisp and golden.

Peel the onions and slice into rings. Dip into milk, then into flour and fry in very hot oil. (Can be deep fried.) Drain well. Serve with coarse salt.

GLAZED IN MUSTARD

1 lb button onions, 3 tablespoons butter, 1 level tablespoon dry mustard, mixed with equal amount of water.

Only attempt this dish when the little onions are available. Peel the onions, leave them whole, and simmer in salted water until half-cooked. Drain. Melt the butter and stir in the mustard. Add the onions. Serve when glazed and coated with the butter-mustard sauce.

ONIONS AND SWEATED TOMATOES

Father considers this one of his masterpieces and surprisingly unusual. Always a howling success. Don't pass it by.

$1\frac{1}{2}$ lb Spanish onions, oil, 1 teaspoon vinegar, $\frac{1}{2}$ teaspoon sugar, origano and/or basil, 3–4 tomatoes, seasoning, 2 tablespoons bottle-top cream.

Slice the onions and separate the rings. Smear your widest frying pan with oil. Add the onions, cover, and simmer over the lowest possible heat. Shake the pan each time you pass it. When the onions begin to soften, add the vinegar, sugar and a good sprinkling of the herbs. By this time there should be quite a bit of liquid sweated out of the onions. Give them a bit of a stir, re-cover the pan, and continue to simmer for a further five minutes.

Meanwhile cut the tomatoes in half. Add them to the pan and arrange side by side, cut side down, so that they rest on a bed of onion. Sprinkle with salt and freshly ground black pepper. Again cover the pan and let the tomatoes sweat. When their skins begin to crinkle they are almost ready. Remove the cover and raise the heat to evaporate most of the liquid.

Just before serving, check the seasoning and pour in the bottle-top cream. This slow cooking brings out the fullest flavour of the vegetables. Total cooking time – 1–1½ hours.

PEAS

Boiled in salty water, sometimes with mint, are very nice and it is difficult to spoil them. They are nicer still if served with a good sprinkling of finely chopped fresh mint and a knob or two of butter, added just before serving. Or try the following:

PEAS, LETTUCE AND ONIONS

The traditionalists will tell you that you should use the heart of a lettuce. Don't be put off if you haven't got one. A few soggy leaves that would shame a salad are a perfectly reasonable substitute. Ideally, you should use baby onions. If they are out of season you won't do too badly with a roughly chopped onion.

6 or more baby onions, butter, 1 lettuce heart, 1 lb packet frozen peas, bayleaf, thyme, parsley, stock, seasoning, 1 egg yolk.

If the button onions are available, peel them and sauté gently in butter until brown and tender. If not, do the same with chunks of a large onion, breaking them up as little as possible but don't let them get too brown. Put your lettuce into a pot with a good quantity of butter. Add the frozen peas, bayleaf, a pinch of thyme and a couple of sprigs of parsley, a little stock or water, and seasoning. (If you manage to get fresh peas, you will need more stock and a longer cooking time.) Add the onions. Cover the pot and simmer for ten minutes by which time the peas should have defrosted and cooked. Shake the pan from time to time otherwise you will finish up with 'peas avec les onions et lettuce à la burned'.

Beat an egg yolk with a tablespoon of water. When the peas are cooked strain any liquid from the pot. Let it cool before adding the egg yolk. This is the tricky bit. Stir that egg in well before returning to the stove. Re-heat slowly. Do not let it boil: the sauce should thicken. If it does you will be serving your vegetables with an egg sauce. If it doesn't and the egg curdles, don't worry. You will now be serving your vegetables with a scrambled egg sauce. It's perfectly acceptable and very pleasant. Before pouring over the vegetables, check seasoning. Remove the bayleaf and sprigs of parsley.

BABY PEAS IN A CREAM SAUCE (PETIT POIS)

Tip peas into melted butter. When the butter has been absorbed, cover with boiling cream. Season. Cook until tender.

PEAS WITH BITS OF THIS AND THAT

Make some little croûtons. Add those to minted cooked peas. Or crispy bits of bacon. Or both.

POTATOES

I have read with great pleasure in a dieticians' tome that a potato contains 70 calories, the same as a good eating apple. I have read elsewhere that the calorie content for the potato is 95 and for the apple 45. Now who am I going to believe? If the first statement is correct, how can a potato be fattening? Is an apple fattening? (Maybe it was a very little potato and a very big apple.)

As it is such an admirable vegetable, I am disposed to accept the first statement and risk my waistline.

Recipes for the potato are many amd imaginative. It is such a versatile vegetable. But they are so often served mashed, roasted, sautéed in too much fat, as chips or as chips or as chips, or as soggy chips. And of course there are the 'lazy cook's masterpieces' – tinned new potatoes or deep frozen croquettes. I hope the following will titillate your taste buds.

POTATOES AND MUSHROOMS

See recipe for Mushrooms and Potatoes on page 48. I place this at the head of affairs as I would hate you to overlook it.

POTATO PIE

Butter, breadcrumbs, nutmeg, 1½ lb mashed potatoes, 3 hard-boiled eggs, ¼–½ lb ham, seasoning.

Butter an oven-proof dish. Sprinkle it with breadcrumbs. Add a good pinch of nutmeg to ordinary mashed potatoes. Spread half the potatoes over the breadcrumbs. Cover with sliced hard-boiled eggs and squares of ham, season and mask with the remainder of the potato. Sprinkle with additional breadcrumbs and dot with butter. Bake in a hot oven until heated through and the breadcrumbs brown (20–30 mins).

If you like a cheese flavour you can add several flat, thinly sliced pieces of cheese to the filling.

SLICED POTATOES

1. Solo

Very simple but worth doing for a change. Butter an oven-proof dish, slice the potatoes and lay the slices in it, one slice overlapping another. Season with salt, freshly ground pepper and a pinch of nutmeg. Dot with butter and bake in a hot oven for an hour. The addition of a little stock is a good idea. It softens the potatoes on the bottom while the ones on the top become crisp and brown. Quantities as required.

2. With Tomatoes and Chopped Onions

Proceed as above. On top of the first layer place a covering of sliced tomatoes and chopped onion. If you have any ham, shred it and add. Or tiny, crisply fried pieces of bacon. Omit any stock, as there should be enough moisture from the tomatoes. Season as you go. Bake in a hot oven for an hour. Quantities as required.

In both the above recipes you can place the oven dish on the bottom shelf as the main meal cooks and remove to the top shelf for a final browning with the heat raised. This means a longer cooking time.

3. With Stock or Milk and Garlic

Slice $1\frac{1}{2}$ lb of potatoes very thinly. Butter an oven dish. Rub it well with garlic. Spread the potatoes, layer upon layer, into the dish. Mix an egg with $1\frac{1}{2}$ cups of stock, seasoning and nutmeg. Pour over the potatoes. The stock should barely cover them. Sprinkle lavishly with grated cheese and bake very slowly in the oven. The best place to put them is on the floor of the oven and allow two hours' cooking time; if cooked on a centre shelf about $1\frac{1}{4}$ hours. You can use milk instead of stock. The result is a kind of baked custard mixed around the potatoes. On the whole I prefer to use stock.

ROAST POTATOES

This is a different way. Using this method, the potatoes will turn out free of fat and crisp on the outside, creamy inside, and is the best way I know to roast a potato.

Choose equal-sized potatoes. Par-boil them, drain. If you haven't peeled them, peel them now. Then very carefully scratch the surface with a fork. Place in a baking dish with very good fat or oil. Roll them around gently until all sides are slightly smeared. Season as you do so. Place on the shelf under the roast. Turn from time to time. Allow $1\frac{1}{2}$ hours of cooking time in the oven.

MASHED POTATOES

Mash them with plenty of butter, milk and seasoning, and Father will then add his little extra:

1. A handful of grated cheese.
2. Mint or parsley.
3. Bits of crispy bacon.
4. Herbs of his choice.
5. Very finely chopped onion.
6. Bits of chopped ham.

NOTE: when mashing, see that heated milk is always used.

POTATO PANCAKE

This is one the kids will like.

1 lb potatoes, butter, seasoning, 1 small finely chopped onion, 2 tomatoes, tablespoon flour, parsley.

Mash the potatoes in butter. Don't use any milk. Season. Add the chopped onion, chopped tomato, flour, and a handful of chopped parsley. Mix well. Lightly oil a flat baking dish (just a smear) and put in the potatoes. Shape into a fairly thick circular round. Brush lightly with melted butter and bake in a hot oven until brown on top.

OR

Shape the potatoes into oblongs, rectangles, triangles etc. It's best to do this with floured hands and your 'shape' can be dipped into more flour to help keep its form. Then fry the shapes in oil until browned on all sides.

I once made a gingerbread man (without ginger of course) out of this mixture. I garnished with sultanas for his face and made a belt out of a strip of green pepper to encircle a bulging belly. Great applause from the kids.

HALF POTATOES

1½ lb potatoes, ½ glass white wine, ½ pint stock, seasoning, herbs, 1 egg.

Par-boil the potatoes. Peel and cut in half. Place in a casserole. Add white wine, stock, seasoning (use a light hand) and a few mild herbs. Cover the casserole and cook in a medium oven for twenty minutes or until the potatoes are tender. Remove. Drain the sauce from the potatoes and thicken with a beaten egg on top of the stove. Keep the heat very low, stir all the time, and don't let it boil. Use a double saucepan if you have one, or less ambitiously thicken with a beurre manié. Pour over the potatoes, garnish and serve.

NEW POTATOES IN SAUCE

1 lb new potatoes, ½ cup Béchamel sauce, parsley, 1 finely chopped onion, seasoning, juice of a lemon, 1 teaspoon French mustard, tarragon, chervil.

Boil the potatoes and when cooked remove the skin if not previously scraped. Make the Béchamel sauce, but one which is not too thick. Add ½ teaspoon of herbs – a mixture of what you have or those named but don't go mad and use sage in this dish. It's too strong. Lean towards the milder herbs – and the onion. Finally, season, add the lemon juice and the French mustard. Pour over the potatoes and garnish.

NEW POTATOES – SOLO

You intended to boil them, dot them with butter, and sprinkle with parsley. Why not? Excellent. Here is a little variation.

Cook the potatoes scraped free of skin and place in your widest pan in which you have already melted a liberal quantity of butter. Turn up the heat and roll the potatoes around until they are browned on all sides. Season as you proceed. Finally add two good handfuls of chopped parsley; let this frizzle in the butter but don't let it burn. You may need extra butter.

JACKET POTATOES

Baked in their skins. A magnificent way to cook them as they then retain most of their goodness. But if you don't like a crisp, well-baked potato skin to crunch, go back to the earlier recipes. I once went into a small café which took pride in their specially prepared, luncheon, jacket potatoes. They did a roaring trade but, to my horror, I noted that half the customers scraped the flesh of the potato and the excellent fillings from the lovingly prepared, crispy, crunchy shells. These were left on the side of their plates.

However for those of you who enjoy a bit of a crunch, herewith a few suggestions. The first crop of the new season's potatoes are no good. Wait until they are bigger and the skins get tougher. A preparatory soaking in milk will help towards a crisp skin.

Cook by placing on the top shelf of a hot oven for at least 1½ hours. Much longer if you are cooking something else in the oven at the same time which requires a slower cooking. Be sure to prick them after an hour, otherwise they might explode.

Having cooked them to your satisfaction, slice off the top or cut in halves without slicing right through. Remove most of the flesh and mix in with one of the following fillings. A little melted butter should always be added except when using cream or any other liquid.

1. Cream and grated cheese.
2. Pieces of chopped ham.
3. Crispy bits of fried bacon.
4. Left-over meat, finely chopped or minced. Add a little nutmeg and a dash of cayenne pepper.
5. Herby potatoes. Choose your own herbs.
6. Chives and crushed garlic.
7. Chopped spicy continental sausage and sour cream (or yoghurt).
8. Chopped mushrooms sautéed in butter. Add a dash of cream. Sautéed onions also.
9. Chopped cooked poultry and almonds.
10. Soft herring roes already cooked in butter, then mixed with bread-crumbs.

The potatoes should either be garnished, or if using a cheese or breadcrumb topping, placed back in the oven or under the grill to brown.

RATATOUILLE

You'll find this recipe or something similar to it in most comprehensive cook books. With tastes widening I feel it should be included.

3 aubergines, 3 red or green peppers, 3 medium onions, 4–5 tomatoes, oil, seasoning.

Cut the unpeeled aubergines into cubes, slice the peppers and onions, chop up the tomatoes. Put plenty of oil (about 5 tablespoons) into a saucepan and add the onions and peppers. Cover and simmer for at least ten minutes. When they begin to soften add the aubergines, and after several more minutes, the tomatoes. Season. Simmer for a further 10–15 mins when most of the oil will have been absorbed. Take the lid off for the last five minutes of cooking. Quantities given are for about six people. You can vary the ingredients to suit yourself although I find the above a satisfactory balance.

RICE

Nothing like rice pudding with curry! How often have you suffered that? I have rarely eaten good long grain rice in a private home but it's perfectly simple to prepare if, like all good cooking, it is done with care. So I'm going to make a bit of a fuss about it. Father's fluffy rice will always be superb.

FLUFFY RICE

1. Boil 2–3 tablespoons long grain rice for each person in a large quantity of water. I hear mutterings: 'Should rinse it first. Gets rid of the starch.' I never bother.

2. When adding the rice to the boiling water (it must be boiling when the rice is put in) stir well as the rice is inclined to stick together. More mutterings: 'Should have rinsed it first.' When the rice grains have separated and the water has returned to boiling point, lower the heat and let it simmer.

3. Go away for 10 minutes and have a drink. Not a moment longer.

4. Uncover and *watch like a hawk*. When the water turns milky, taste. Not cooked. Don't go away.

5. Taste again. Perfect. Soft on the outside and slightly nutty inside (*Al dente*). This is the moment of truth, as they say in all the best novels. If it cooks a moment longer, all will be lost. Cooking time, once the water re-boils, should be between 10 and 12 minutes, depending on the quality of the rice.

6. Strain.

7. Wash well in either hot or cold water. The purists are aghast. Hot water! It has to be cold. (I find hot works just as well, especially if I'm in a hurry.)

8. When well-rinsed and drained, spread on a wide pan and place in the oven. The oven should be fairly warm and will re-heat the rice. I cheat. I leave the gas on gas mark 1 or 2. It's quicker. But every minute or so, drag a fork through the rice to fluff it up. Don't use a spoon, it will crush the grains. Fluff often if you are going to leave the gas on, otherwise it *will* dry and harden and the mutterings will turn into hysterically triumphant screams of 'I told you so.'

The rice should be perfect if these instructions are followed carefully.

ANOTHER METHOD OF COOKING RICE

Ideal for a pilaff or paella, and the only method to be used if making a risotto. Apart from these, I always use the first method and add a little oil later if it seems necessary.

Tip the rice into a quantity of oil and heat until translucent. Cover with boiling water or stock. Season. The quantities are two parts of water to one of rice measured by volume. When the liquid has been absorbed the rice should be cooked. If not, add more water or stock. It sounds simple, but not as simple as the preceding method. The rice can burn if not stirred frequently, be overcooked or too greasy.

If making a risotto, use only the plump fat Italian rice. It should be creamy and a little moist. It shouldn't be dry.

FRIED RICE

I've tried all kinds of ways to get fried rice to look and taste as it is in most Chinese restaurants. I've put oil into a pan, added the rice, cooked slow, cooked fast, and finished up with a rather nasty mess.

So I was going to suggest that should you fancy a Chinese meal with fried rice, give your wife a treat and take her out to dinner. But at last I've succeeded. My better half presented me with a non-stick frying pan of ample proportions. Invitations to dine out at a Chinese restaurant are now limited.

Boil the rice in salted water as for fluffy rice and rinse in cold water. Drain. Put a good smearing of oil in your non-stick pan. Chop up an onion and throw that in. Cook gently until softened. Then add the rice. Give it a good stir and watch carefully. Every now and then, there will be a little pop as the rice fries. Keep stirring sporadically until all the oil is absorbed.

Remember that 'fried rice' doesn't mean that the rice should turn brown or burn. It should be more glazed than anything. Add more oil if you think it is required.

To make Father's Special Fried Rice, beat up one or two eggs. Pour into the pan and wait five seconds before beginning to stir in. They should have started to congeal by then and will mix into the rice in scraggy yellow bits. Add a few prawns if you have them. Chop up the top of a spring onion into tiny circular pieces and sprinkle over the rice before serving – or add anything else green and suitable as a colour contrast.

RICE FOR CURRY

Boiled fluffy rice, of course.

Of course: but with Father's imagination, he's going to present his Superior Rice for Curry which would cost pounds if bought in an Indian restaurant. It would probably be sold as Rice Pilau or Berani Rice.

The secret? He's going to turn it yellow, golden yellow, yellowy brown, or rust coloured depending on which spices he uses or how colour blind you are. Extra ingredients needed are spices such as cumin, coriander, cardamom seeds, turmeric, mace, etc. Hard-boiled eggs, slices of tomato and wedges of lemon.

You can use all, or some, of the spices. 1–2 tablespoons turmeric is essential to change the rice's colour. Add to the boiling salted water before you put the rice in to cook. If using the other spices such as cumin etc., warm them first, then crush them in a pestle and mortar, and add. These will give extra flavour.

When the rice is cooked, rinse as little as possible to avoid washing away surface spices although the rice will have absorbed most of their flavour. When dried, and nice and fluffy, spread on a serving plate so that it is slightly domed. Garnish with hard-boiled eggs, quartered or sliced tomatoes, wedges of lemon, and bits of green such as the tiny rounds of spring onions mentioned in the preceding recipe. It will look superb and appetising and is well worth the effort.

BUTTERED RICE

Melt two tablespoons of butter for each ½ lb rice. Don't let it brown. Remove from the heat, let it cool for a moment, then mix in a beaten egg. Stir this egg butter sauce into hot, fluffy cooked rice.

ORANGE RICE

1 cup long grain rice, 1 cup diced celery, 3 tablespoons chopped green pepper, 3 tablespoons finely chopped onion, 2 tablespoons shredded orange rind, 3–4 tablespoons butter, ½ cup orange juice, salt.

Cook the rice in salted water as described for fluffy rice (page 56). Sauté the finely chopped vegetables and the grated orange rind in butter until tender. Then add a drop of water, orange juice and a sprinkling of salt. Bring to the boil and simmer until the liquid is reduced by half. Mix into the rice and let it stand for five minutes in a warm oven before serving.

You can use more orange juice if it appeals to you. I find this a magnificent rice and is best served with duck or pork (see pork recipe, page 90).

SPINACH

SPINACH AND FISH

Father is convinced Popeye failed and put the kids off spinach. He didn't have Father's recipe. Have you got four oven-proof soup plates? If so, proceed.

1 lb cooked white fish, 1 x 12 oz. packet of frozen spinach (or 2 lb fresh spinach), salt, butter, juice ½ lemon, nutmeg, 1 finely chopped onion, ½ cup double cream, sliced tomatoes, grated cheese, paprika.

Flake the fish. Heat the spinach. Add to it salt, a good dollop of butter, lemon juice, and a pinch nutmeg. (If using fresh spinach, wash thoroughly, place in pot with 1–2 tablespoons water or stock, salt to taste, dollop of butter, lemon juice and pinch nutmeg. As the spinach sinks down in the pot slash at it with a sharp knife. Boil until the liquid has almost completely evaporated. Strain in colander. Give it another good slash until cut very fine. Press any excess liquid out of it.) Boil the onion in a little water until tender. Strain.

Put alternate layers of fish and spinach into each bowl. Add a further touch of nutmeg to each layer of spinach. Mix the onion into the cream and pour equal amounts into each bowl. Cover with sliced tomatoes, a liberal sprinkling of grated cheese and finally a decorative pinch or two of paprika. Bake in a moderately hot oven for about 25 minutes until well heated through and the cheese has begun to melt. Finish by browning under the grill. If attempting to brown in the oven place the dishes on the top shelf and turn up the heat.

Don't tell the kids what's in it. Give it a name. Say, 'Poisson avec le grande Surpris du Pa.' They'll be surprised all right. They'll be into the spinach before they know what has happened to them.

CHINESE-TYPE SPINACH

Another one Popeye missed. He never got to China.

2 lb spinach, 6 tablespoons oil, 1 finely chopped onion, 1 tablespoon fresh chopped ginger (or 1 heaped teaspoon ginger powder), 2 pinches sugar, 2–3 cloves crushed garlic, $\frac{1}{4}$ cup strong chicken stock, 2 tablespoons soy sauce, $1\frac{1}{2}$ tablespoons sherry, salt.

Chop the spinach roughly and throw into heated oil. Give it a stir, then add onion, ginger (powdered ginger will do but it is not nearly as good), sugar, garlic and stock. Another little stir. All this is done over a strong heat. Cook for 1–2 minutes. Then pour in the soy sauce and sherry. Salt to taste as you cook. Stir gently all the time. Total cooking time – say 8–10 minutes.

SPINACH A LA ORDINAIRE

Included just to stop you boiling it in salted water.

2 lb spinach, 2 tablespoons butter, 2 tablespoons stock, seasoning, nutmeg, 2 teaspoons lemon juice.

Wash thoroughly. Put in large pot with half the butter, and the stock. Cover. Cook over moderate heat until you can cut it with a knife in the pot. Season. That should take anything from 10 to 15 minutes depending on the youth of the spinach. Remove, drain, and squeeze out excess liquid. Heat the rest of the butter in a frying pan. In with the spinach and nutmeg and stir for 2 minutes. Sprinkle with the lemon juice and serve.

Or alternatively, omit the lemon juice; place instead in a heatproof shallow dish, sprinkle with $\frac{1}{2}$ cup grated cheese and brown under the grill.

CHAPTER 5

Something Fishy

The fishy thing about this section is where do you get fresh fish unless you are lucky enough to live near an unpolluted river or the sea. Freshness in fish is, of course, the first and most important essential.

So I've limited the recipes in this section. They are mostly for white fish such as cod and haddock which deep freeze reasonably well and can be uncommonly good if cooked with enterprise and imagination. Recipes for most shell fish and the like have, on the whole, been omitted because they have become so expensive.

However, should you be lucky enough to catch a sea monster yourself, or that massive trout which has lurked in a nearby river for months, clean it, poach it in a court bouillon, fry it in clarified butter, or grill it. Don't risk this prize by smothering it in a distracting sauce. Prepare it simply. If it really is a monster, bake it in the oven.

COD AND PEARS

4 cod steaks, 3 tablespoons butter, 1 onion, $\frac{1}{2}$ cup of white wine, juice $\frac{1}{2}$ lemon, 1 small tin tomatoes, $1\frac{1}{2}$ tablespoons tomato purée, 1 green pepper, 6 stoned green olives, 1 tablespoon chopped parsley, seasoning, 2 pears.

You can use cod fillets instead but they are not so easy to handle.

Place the steaks in a heat-proof buttered pan which can be covered. Sprinkle the fish with chopped onion. Pour in the wine and the lemon juice. Cover and simmer for 10 minutes. Remove the steaks carefully and keep warm. Reduce the remaining liquid by rapid boiling. Add the tomatoes and the tomato purée, thinly sliced green pepper, the olives well chopped, and the parsley. Season and simmer until well amalgamated. Peel, core and slice the pears into chunks. Add to the sauce and return the fish to the pan. Cook slowly for a further 10 minutes or until the pears begin to soften. Serve garnished with sprigs of parsley.

COD OR HADDOCK IN SOUR CREAM

$1\frac{1}{2}$ lb cod or haddock, butter, flour, 8 mushrooms, seasoning, 2 hard-boiled eggs, 5–6 tablespoons sour cream.

Cut the fish into even-sized chunks. Dry them and dip in seasoned flour. Fry slowly in butter for about 10 minutes depending on the size of the chunks. When cooked place in a shallow heat-proof dish. Slice the mushrooms and sauté in butter. Don't forget to season them. Spread over the fish together with sliced hard-boiled eggs. Add about 1 teaspoon flour to the pan in which the mushrooms were cooked thus making a little roux. If all the butter has been absorbed by the mushrooms add a little more. Add the sour cream. Stir until thickened and smooth. Pour over the fish mushrooms and eggs. Sprinkle with cheese and brown under grill.

CUTTLEFISH, SQUID AND INKFISH

You can buy them now in many of the ambitious supermarkets. Something different to try – once you get over their revolting appearance and pluck up the courage to clean them. Very tasty.

They come under all kinds of names and sizes, e.g. calamaretti, seppie, calamari etc. Just ask for squid or inkfish. If they are small they are usually cleaned, cut into rings, dipped in batter or flour, fried in oil until crisp and served with slices of lemon. If larger they are quite often stewed.

To clean, cut out the ink bag, remove the intestines and the spine bone. Wash well. You should then have something pleasant and milky white. Beware of the long-bodied varieties – they are likely to be very tough and may require hours of stewing.

1.   Fried

Buy some small ones, clean, cut into rings as described above, and fry or deep fry. Offer them as an hors d'oeuvre with some fresh bread and butter, and chunks of lemon. Or put them in a paella or in any mixed fish dish.

2.   Stewed Cuttlefish, Inkfish or Squid

If you've bought a big one or several small ones weighing, when cleaned, at least 1 lb, prepare as above. Sauté two chopped onions in oil. Then add the cuttlefish dusted with seasoned flour. They can brown slightly. Next add a glass of red wine and enough water to cover the molluscs and onions. Continue by adding a little water to the rapidly vanishing wine, a crushed clove of garlic, a small tin of tomatoes, 1 dessertspoon of tomato purée and seasoning. Cover the pan and stew very slowly for $1\frac{1}{2}$–2 hours. If there is too much liquid left when finally cooked, reduce by fast boiling.

Serve with rice or chunks of lightly toasted bread.

FISH COCKTAIL

There is a monstrosity served in many restaurants and often at private dinner parties which is called prawn cocktail. This revolting concoction invariably consists of a few wilting lettuce leaves, 3–4 cotton-wool deep-frozen prawns, and a thick goo of bottle mayonnaise mixed with tomato ketchup and Worcestershire sauce. And the price is monstrous too. Thus prejudiced, I offer no recipe for this famous (or infamous) hors d'oeuvre. If you manage to get genuinely fresh prawns, by all means make one.

The sauce which follows with the fish cocktail should please.

Mayonnaise, double cream, tobasco or chilli powder, tomato purée, Worcestershire sauce, cayenne pepper, freshly cooked fish, crisp lettuce, watercress. Quantities as required.

First make a thick mayonnaise (see page 122). Add to it a portion of whipped double cream (2–3 tablespoons to 1 cup mayonnaise). Then add tobasco (or chilli powder first mixed to a paste in a little water or oil), tomato purée, Worcestershire sauce, and cayenne pepper according to taste.

Flake the freshly cooked fish. Line stemmed glasses with crisp lettuce leaves. Add the fish, cover with mayonnaise and garnish with watercress. Chill before serving.

This will not be as good as a *first-class* prawn cocktail, but it is a comparatively inexpensive and delicious substitute.

HALIBUT AND BANANAS

1½ lb halibut fillets, flour, egg, breadcrumbs, flaked almonds, 2 bananas, 2–3 tablespoons butter.

Cut the fish into smallish pieces, egg and breadcrumb them after first dusting in salted flour. Deep fry for 6 minutes in hot fat. Toast a good handful of flaked or chopped almonds until lightly browned. Cut the bananas slantwise. Arrange the fish on a serving plate surrounded by the bananas. Melt the butter and pour over the fish. Sprinkle with the toasted almonds.

HALIBUT WITH CIDER OR WHITE WINE

1½ lb halibut fillets, 2 tablespoons butter, 1 chopped onion, 2 cloves of chopped garlic, 1½ tablespoons flour, 1 cup white wine or cider, juice 1 lemon, salt, pinch cayenne pepper, chopped parsley.

Dust the fillets in salted flour and fry in a pan smeared with oil for 3 minutes on each side. Place in an oven dish. Melt the butter which can be mixed into any remaining oil and lightly fry the onion and garlic. Sprinkle in the flour and amalgamate to make an onion-garlic roux. Pour in the wine and lemon juice. Stir until the sauce is smooth – apart from the the pieces of onion, of course. Season the sauce with salt and a pinch of cayenne pepper. Pour over the fish and bake in a hot oven until the fish is completely cooked. This should only take a few more minutes. Garnish with chopped parsley.

HADDOCK FISH CHOWDER

This is a very heavy fish soup. Served with fresh, crisp French bread, your family is greedier than mine if they can eat anything else when they've finished – except perhaps a little fruit. Simple and inexpensive.

1 onion, 2 rashers of bacon, butter, 1 lb haddock, 1 large tin tomatoes, 1 pint of light stock, bayleaf, 2 cloves, ½–¾ lb of potatoes, Parmesan.

Chop up the onion and the bacon, sauté in butter. Cube the fish. Mush up the tomatoes and tip into a saucepan together with 1 pint stock, a bayleaf, the cloves, the bacon, onion and fish. Season. Cut the potatoes into chunky pieces and add these. Simmer the lot for about twenty minutes with the pot covered. Remove the lid for the last five minutes. Keep the heat low so that the potato pieces and the fish don't break up.

Before serving, remove the bayleaf and the cloves if you can find them. Serve in soup bowls with Parmesan cheese. (Some people prefer it without the cheese.) Try a green salad on the side. Cucumber and sour cream (see page 32) is excellent for this.

GRILLED HERRINGS

Herrings for four, flour, oil, French mustard, breadcrumbs, seasoning, butter.

Clean and scale the fish if necessary. Make two or three incisions on each side with a sharp knife. Dip in seasoned flour. Place on a well-oiled piece of foil and brush the topsides of the fish with more oil. Grill, 2–3 minutes on each side. Remove the fish from the foil which is used as a kind of platter to stop the fish breaking up. Place in a gratin dish. Spread liberally with French mustard. Sprinkle with breadcrumbs, season and dot with butter. Bake high up in a very hot oven for a further five minutes.

NOTE: If you can get your dish under the grill without it cracking, you could finish the cooking there.

MACKEREL

Not a fish I would cook at home unless I'd caught it myself. By the time they arrive at the fishmongers, their eyes are often glazed and rigor mortis has set in. Let me assume therefore that you have managed to get some fresh mackerel, for fresh they must be.

1.   In Black Butter Sauce

Poach the cleaned fish in salted water for forty minutes. Remove the backbone if preparing for guests, otherwise let the family show their expertise. Place the fish on a hot dish. Sprinkle with capers and grated cheese. Boiled potatoes are an adequate accompaniment.

Black butter sauce is made as follows. Four parts butter to two parts vinegar. Melt the butter until it starts to turn brown, not black despite its name. Pour over the fish. In the same pan, pour the vinegar which will immediately sizzle. Raise the heat and reduce by half. Pour this over the fish. Serve as quickly as possible.

2.   In Red Wine

Fillet small mackerel – enough for four. Simmer in a court bouillon consisting of half a bottle of red wine, the same quantity of water, a chopped onion, a bayleaf, a pinch of thyme and a sprig of parsley. Depending on the thickness of the fillets, the cooking time will take about 15 minutes. When cooked, keep hot in a little of the liquor. Strain the rest of the liquor and reduce to half its volume by rapid boiling. Thicken this sauce with a beurre manié. Remove the fillets and place on a serving dish. Add the liquor in which they have been kept warm to the thickened sauce. Stir in and pour over the fish. Garnish.

MUSSELS

These are harder to buy as the wet fish shops disappear and supermarkets seem loath to handle them. Whatever you do, don't buy bottled or tinned ones; they must be fresh. And even if there is an R in the month, you can eat them without dire consequences despite rumours to the contrary. I offer two recipes. The first one, with all kinds of minute variations, will no doubt be familiar to you.

1.   Moules à la Marinière

That's fresh mussels cooked in wine and water, or all wine if Father hasn't been at the bottle.

1 quart mussels for each person (less if served as a first course), 1 cup white wine or white wine and water, 1 chopped onion or the white of a leek, chopped parsley.

Wash the mussels thoroughly and shave off their beards with a sharp knife. Discard those which are broken but don't close when touched. Sling into a wide pot with the onion or leek. Add the cup of liquid, cover the pot and heat gently. When all the shells open, the mussels are cooked. Strain the liquid carefully, preferably through muslin as it can be gritty if you haven't washed the mussels thoroughly. Discard any which have refused to open. Leave in their shells or you can take them out altogether. Place in soup bowls. See that the liquor is quite hot, add some chopped parsley and pour equal amounts into each bowl. Sop up sauce with chunks of crusty French bread. (NOTE: If you would like more liquid, increase quantities of wine and water – or you could use a light stock.)

2. Mussels, Mushrooms and Prawns

4 dozen mussels, $\frac{1}{4}$ lb sliced mushrooms, $1\frac{1}{2}$ tablespoons butter, $\frac{1}{2}$ cup white wine, 3 tablespoons cream, prawns, 1 tablespoon chopped parsley, seasoning, breadcrumbs.

For four people, use one dozen mussels each. Prepare and cook them as in the preceding recipe. Take the mussels out of their shells and keep warm. Sauté the mushrooms in butter. When softened sprinkle with flour, mix well and stir in the strained liquor slowly. Then add the cream. When you have a smooth sauce, add a few prawns and finally the mussels, the chopped parsley and season. Pour into a buttered heat-proof dish, sprinkle with breadcrumbs and dot with butter. Brown under the grill.

PRAWNS IN CHILLI SAUCE

1 lb prawns is required. Sounds expensive, but the total cost for four is less than a joint of beef, much less than a couple of pounds of choice grilling steak, and not much more than a shoulder of lamb. In fact, it will satisfy the hunger pangs of five or six people. Make it go further by cooking extra rice.

2 tablespoons butter, 1 chopped onion, 1 stick celery, 1 green pepper, seasoning, 1 dessertspoon flour, 1 pint stock, 1 teaspoon sugar, 1 teaspoon white vinegar, white wine (optional), chilli powder or tabasco sauce, 1 lb peeled prawns, 3–4 tomatoes, 1 cup of cooked peas.

Melt the butter in a wide pan which can be covered. Sauté together onion, celery pieces cut in inch lengths, strips of green and/or red pepper, and season. When partly cooked, sprinkle with flour, stir well. Add the stock slowly, then the sugar, the vinegar (or 2 teaspoons lemon juice), white wine (optional but what you can spare up to $\frac{3}{4}$ cup) and finally the tabasco or chilli powder. I haven't put in quantities as they are very fiery ingredients and it is a matter of personal taste, so proceed with caution. I suggest 2 tablespoons of tabasco or, at most to start with, 1 level tablespoon of chilli powder mixed with a little water to form a paste. Some brands will remove the roof of your mouth. When the sauce is well mixed and smooth (it shouldn't be too thick) check seasoning. If not hot enough, add more tabasco or chilli powder.

Finally add the frozen prawns (it is better not to defrost them first), the quartered tomatoes and the peas. The tomatoes should merely be heated through rather than well cooked. Serve with rice.

You can use more celery and an extra pepper to stretch this colourful, delicious meal.

PA'S PAELLA

There are a few great dishes in the world which are fairly simple to cook. High on my list would come Roast Beef and Yorkshire pudding, Steak and Kidney pie, Beef Stroganoff and Spanish Paella. Although the last may be fairly simple to prepare in Spain, it's not so easy to make in this country. Some of the ingredients are difficult to get and how many of us have a proper paella dish? You'll need a little help if only to clean up the mess as you proceed. There are many kinds of paella but I would never attempt one without some chicken, pork and shell fish (or squid).

ESSENTIAL INGREDIENTS:

1 pint mussels, and/or prawns, chicken stock, rice, chicken pieces, 2 strips belly of pork or salt pork, oil, garlic, seasoning, tomatoes.

You can add what you like from the following:

OPTIONAL INGREDIENTS:

White wine, saffron, peas, squid, octopus, crayfish instead of the prawns, bits of fish, spicy continental sausage.

Try the top lot first. Experiment later.

Scrub the mussels. Put in a pot. If you've bought unpeeled prawns, peel most of them and throw the heads and shells in as well. They will improve the flavour of the mussel stock. Add a little water and left-over white wine (optional). Bring to the boil with the lid on. When the mussels open, they're cooked. When they don't open they're bad: discard. Strain the liquid from the pot into another large pot with a good quantity of chicken stock. Cook patna rice in this liquid (2 tablespoons per person). If using saffron, add with the rice. Much better with saffron but it is terribly expensive. (See page 56 for cooking fluffy rice.) Strain and dry as directed.

I hear a wail of protest. The rice should be put into a pan containing a little oil, heated through until translucent, and stock added to be absorbed by the rice by the time it is cooked. True. That is the principle generally used to cook a genuine Spanish paella in a genuine Spanish paella dish. But we haven't got one, have we?

So using the fluffy rice method, please continue. Dry it in the oven.

You will notice that strict quantities have not been given. It is a marvellous dish for imagination and flair! Use what you like subject to the note about essential ingredients. I suggest 3 joints of chicken (legs and thighs) cut into four pieces, and a dozen chunky cubes of belly of pork. Fry these together in oil and garlic until the chicken pieces are cooked and lightly browned (20–25 mins over a medium heat). Season. Add the prawns towards the end of the cooking to give them time to heat through. Reserve a few in their shells for garnish.

Cook some peas and quarter some tomatoes.

Take the rice from the oven and spread over your widest serving dish. It should be heat-proof as it has to go back in the oven – a broad-based gratin dish is ideal. Mix the chicken pieces, pork, peas, prawns and whatever else you've gallantly prepared such as squid or octopus, into the rice. You can stir in 1 tablespoon of oil if you like. Return to the oven (low heat) for 5–10 minutes.

The mussels, which should have been kept warm, are not added until the last five minutes. They will become dry and tough if exposed to oven heat for too long. Remove most of them from their shells and bury them in the rice. Garnish with the remainder in their shells together with the few unpeeled prawns. Return to the oven for a further five minutes or so until everything is well heated through. When all is ready decorate with the tomatoes and a few wedges of lemon.

GRILLED SOLE AND A SIMPLE SAUCE

Butter, parsley, mint, fillets of sole, onion, white wine, seasoning. Quantities are as required.

Mix about 2 tablespoons butter with 1 tablespoon chopped parsley and 2 tablespoons mint. Make incisions in the fillets and press this mixture into each cut. Turn carefully when grilling, about five minutes on each side.

Sauté a finely chopped onion in butter. Don't let it brown. Add a small glass of white wine and a little water. Let it reduce slowly after seasoning gently. Pour over the grilled fish.

Whole fish can be used for this recipe – if you can afford them – but they should be skinned first.

WHITE FISH GRATIN

This one works with most white fish – even coley. But the more delicate the fish, the better. I suggest plaice or lemon sole.

1 lb fish fillets, 6–8 mushrooms, 2 tablespoons butter, 1 tablespoon flour, ½ cup milk, 4 tablespoons single or double cream, seasoning, a few prawns, (optional: white wine), breadcrumbs.

Lay the fillets in a well-buttered heat-proof gratin dish. Sauté sliced mushrooms in most of the butter. When partly cooked, sprinkle with flour. (If using double cream, only use ½ tablespoon.) Mix well. Add the milk, stirring all the time, then the cream so that you finish up with a thickish smooth sauce laced with mushrooms. Season. Now add what prawns you have available – up to sixteen. Bring to the boil. When it bubbles, add that little bit of white wine that you haven't drunk, having first heated it in a separate pot. This is to remove any possibility of the cream curdling, a precaution worth noting when making any wine-cream sauce. Check seasoning. Then pour the sauce of prawns and mushrooms over the fish. Sprinkle with breadcrumbs and dot with the remaining butter. Bake in a moderate oven for thirty minutes. If the breadcrumbs fail to brown finish under the grill.

OR

Sprinkle with both grated cheese and breadcrumbs and dot with butter. It depends on what you are going to serve with the fish.

WHITE FISH WITH A SHARP EGG SAUCE

Fillets of fish for four, seasoning, 1 chopped clove garlic, 4 chopped gherkins, chopped parsley, 1 tablespoon flour, 2 tablespoons butter, $\frac{1}{2}$ cup white wine and water, 1 egg, 1 tablespoon vinegar.

Dust the fish with seasoned flour. Fry in butter until browned and cooked. Remove from the pan and place on a serving dish. Keep warm.

Make the sauce by first frying the garlic gently. Add the chopped gherkins and at the last moment a handful of chopped parsley. Don't let the parsley frizzle. Mix well together and sprinkle with the flour to make a roux. Add the wine and water slowly until it is thick and smooth. Cool. Beat an egg together with the vinegar. Add this to the sauce away from the stove. Return to a low heat, stirring all the time. The sauce should finish like thick mayonnaise. Do not let it boil. Pour over the fish. Garnish with extra chopped gherkins and parsley.

WHITE FISH BAKED IN MUSTARD

1 x 3 lb white fish, 2 teaspoons dry mustard, $\frac{1}{2}$ cup dry white wine, 2 tablespoons oil, 3 tablespoons chopped spring onion, chopped parsley, seasoning.

This is not worth doing unless you are preparing a meal for five or six people, in which case you will need a 3 lb fish after it has been cleaned and beheaded. Score it and place in an oven dish.

Mix the mustard in a little hot water and add to the wine (or less white wine, with lemon juice and water to make $\frac{1}{2}$ cup of liquid), oil, onion, and a handful of chopped parsley. Season to taste. Pour over the fish and bake in a slow oven for 30–40 minutes or until the fish flakes. Test with a fork. Baste continuously. If the liquid evaporates too much, top up with a little water.

When the fish is cooked place it on a serving dish and pour the sauce over it.

WHITE FISH WITH NOODLES

1 lb fish goes a long way with this recipe.

1 lb cod or haddock, $\frac{1}{2}$ lb noodles, 1 leek, 2 tablespoons butter, $1\frac{1}{2}$ cups milk, seasoning, 1 tablespoon flour, cheese.

Boil the fish pieces and keep warm. Boil the noodles in salted water and keep warm. Cut the white part of a leek into thin rounds and sauté very gently in half the butter for six or seven minutes. Add the milk, season lightly, cover the pot and simmer for a further ten minutes. Add flour to make a beurre manié and thicken the milk-leek sauce. Check the seasoning.

Pour half the sauce into a heat-proof oven dish, cover with the fish, then the strained noodles, then the remainder of the sauce. Sprinkle with cheese and brown in a hot oven, or heat through in the oven and brown under the grill.

WHITE FISH WITH WINE AND SULTANAS

1 onion, 1 stick celery, 1 leek (optional), 1 tablespoon parsley, 2 cups water, 1 bayleaf, freshly ground black pepper, juice $\frac{1}{2}$ lemon, $\frac{1}{2}$ cup white wine, 2 tablespoons vinegar, $\frac{1}{2}$ cup of sultanas, $1\frac{1}{4}$ lb white fish fillets, 1 tablespoon butter, 1 tablespoon flour, salt.

Chop up the onion, celery, leek and parsley. Place in a wide frying pan which can be covered. Simmer for twenty minutes in water with a bayleaf and freshly ground black pepper, strain and return liquid to pan. Add the lemon juice, the wine, the vinegar and half the sultanas, bring to the boil, then add the fish. If the liquid doesn't cover the fish, add more water. Simmer covered for 10–15 minutes. Meanwhile, pour a little boiling water over the remaining sultanas to plump them up.

Remove the fish, keep it warm and strain the liquid again. Return this liquid to the pan and reduce to 1 cupful by fast boiling. Then thicken by using a beurre manié made out of the butter and flour, add salt to taste. Pour the sauce over the fish and garnish with the remaining sultanas after removing them from the boiling water.

If the sauce isn't sharp enough add a little more lemon juice.

CHAPTER 6

Marvellous Meat

The important thing to remember about meat is that its juices should be sealed in. That's what most good cook books say, and that's what this good cook book says. Splendid advice, never to be ignored if you've purchased fresh chilled meat and not deep frozen.

The flavour of the meat is in the blood and, in the case of a good steak, also in the fat. This is a problem if using deep-frozen meat. Defrost it and the blood runs out, and all that goodness and flavour is wasted! So if I am using pieces of tough old stewing steak, I don't bother to defrost it. I throw it into boiling water which gives it some kind of sealing, and it gradually defrosts over a low heat. Try it. I've persuaded myself it improves the flavour, and even if it bleeds, the blood mixes into the stock.

The moral of the above is that you should try to avoid buying frozen meat (or using your own deep-freeze meat) if you hope to serve it rare or medium-rare. This applies particularly to beef.

I wouldn't worry too much about lamb. If thawed slowly and allowed to stand in room temperature for an hour or two, it doesn't suffer much and, despite some loss of blood, generally remains excellent. This applies particularly to New Zealand lamb which, after all, is shipped chilled rather than frozen.

FATHER'S BEEFY METHODS

BEEF STROGONOFF

How this great meal has been abused! I've had chuck steak, shin of beef stewed, and on one occasion minced meat smothered in a ghastly goo of thickened sour cream, a squirt of tomato paste, a few mushrooms and a chopped onion which my hostess dared to present as a strogonoff. Fillet steak is the traditional cut for this dish. It's expensive as we all know. I prefer to use one of the cuts suggested below: I find they have more flavour than fillet, *provided* they are not overcooked.

1 lb steak, 2 onions, a lot of butter, $\frac{1}{2}$ lb mushrooms, flour, $\frac{3}{4}$ cup sour cream, $\frac{1}{4}$ cup of yoghurt, seasoning, cup of white wine (optional).

Try using top rump, butcher's fillet (often called feather steak), the eye of the bladebone, back rib fillet or bola steak. (You'll have to have a good butcher to get the latter – one conversant with Kosher cuts.) All are considerably cheaper than fillet.

Having made a choice, cut the meat into thin longish strips (about $2'' \times \frac{1}{4}''$). Remove any fat in the process. Chop up the onions and sauté until soft in a lot of butter. When nearly cooked, but not brown, add the mushrooms and cook until soft. Remove onions and mushrooms and set aside. Add another good dollop of butter to the pan and its juices; the more butter you use the better. Risk a heart attack.

Now for the moment of truth, and this is where most cooks go wrong. When the butter is melted, throw in the strips of meat. Turn them as quickly as you can in the foaming butter until they are no more than sealed on the outside. Keep the heat down while you do this. Don't worry if all the meat has not turned brown and a few bits of red are still showing. Total cooking time should not take more than a minute. If you follow these instructions carefully the meat should keep its maximum flavour. Remove. Keep warm. Sprinkle a teaspoon of flour into the remaining butter and pan juices. It will make the sauce a little thicker. Otherwise omit.

Return the onions and mushrooms to the pan and pour in the sour cream and yoghurt. (Alternatives: all cream, all yoghurt, or a combination of both in any proportion up to the prescribed cupful.) Season. Use plenty of freshly ground black pepper. Finally add a little white wine when the cream begins to bubble. Check seasoning and return the meat to the pan. Mix well. If the sauce turns out to be thicker than you would like, thin by adding milk.

Serve with fluffy rice.

GRILLED OR FRIED STEAK

Slap under the grill topped with a bit of butter, or chuck into a frying pan with oil or butter and cook. Everybody knows how to do this, even the kids. But the following are three memorable recipes to save money. They are masterpieces of deceit. On average these cuts will be anything from a third to fifty per cent cheaper. (Read the notes at the head of the Beef Strogonoff recipe.)

Poor Man's Fillet Mignon

For this you need the eye of the bladebone or back rib fillet. The bladebone has a tiny bit of gristle running across its centre. With a bit of luck you can hide it under the sauce. Back rib fillet is more expensive.

4 pieces of steak, oil, seasoning, 4 rounds fried bread, 8 mushrooms, $1\frac{1}{2}$ tablespoons butter, 1 tablespoon flour, $\frac{1}{2}$ cup beef stock, $\frac{1}{2}$ cup white wine, tomato purée, liver sausage or pâté (optional).

You need one steak for each person, as near to circular in shape as possible, about $1-1\frac{1}{2}$ inches thick. Brush with oil and freshly ground black pepper about an hour before cooking. Heat a thick frying pan and put the meat in without any extra oil. Seal both sides and cook for five to seven minutes on each side: the time will depend on the thickness of the pieces which should be served not more than medium-rare.

Meanwhile make four circular croûtons by frying white bread in a good quantity of oil until both sides are golden brown. When the meat has been cooked, place one steak on a piece of fried bread. Keep warm while you make the sauce. Or, if you're clever, make the sauce while the meat is cooking.

Sauté the mushrooms in the butter. If very small don't slice them. Sprinkle with the flour. Stir gently so that the flour amalgamates with the remaining melted butter and mushroom juices. Add the stock and white wine. Let it bubble gently for a moment. Then add the tomato purée.

If using liver sausage, which is optional, the flavour is improved if it has been gently warmed by placing it on a dish over simmering water.

Place a steak and the fried bread on a heated plate. Top with the liver sausage if being used. Then cover with the sauce, garnish and present. (You could crown each little mountain with half of a small tomato – it's very impressive.)

Should your guests come across that tiny bit of gristle they won't say a word. They'll think you have an inferior butcher but will be too polite to comment. After all, why should they. They will be consuming an excellent meal.

Wine Steak

1½ lb steak, 2 tablespoons butter, 1 finely chopped onion, 1 cup rough red plonk, a drop or two of vinegar, seasoning, 1 tablespoon cream, chopped parsley.

You can use top rump or bola (see page 75) for this one; don't have the steak cut too thickly. Fry in butter, three minutes on each side. Remove and keep warm. Fry the onion in the pan juices. When soft, but not brown, add the wine and the vinegar. Season. Reduce by half by fast boiling. Return the steaks to steep in this sauce for a minute or two before adding the cream (bottle-top cream will do). Turn the steaks over once or twice over a low heat until they are thoroughly hot. Serve, garnished with parsley. You'll find the sauce roughish and full flavoured – excellent if the steak is suspect.

Steak with Tomato and Garlic Sauce

1½ lb steak, 1 small can Italian tomatoes, oil, origano or basil, 2 cloves garlic, seasoning.

Fry the steaks until cooked to your satisfaction. Make the sauce while the steaks cook. Tip a can of tomatoes into a saucepan containing a very little oil. Sprinkle with a pinch of origano and/or basil. Add two finely chopped garlic cloves. Heat slowly until most of the liquid has evaporated. Season to taste. The sauce should be thickish. Spread over the steak and serve garnished. Don't go out afterwards: the garlic content is fresh and strong. A good sauce, if your meat is inclined to be tough or flavourless.

Fresh tomatoes can be used instead of canned ones. They will require a longer cooking.

ROAST BEEF

I'm sure you all know how to cook one of the greatest meals on earth. Roast Beef and Yorkshire Pud. Two heartfelt pleas, however. Please don't wreck the joint by overcooking. It *has* to be at least pink in the middle. Second plea: try buying a wing rib or a joint on the bone rather than the more popular rolled round of beef. You should find the flavour and tenderness of these kinds of cuts generally better, although the following recipe can only be cooked with a rolled round of beef!

Father's Special Roast Beef

2½–3 lb round of beef, 2 onions, 2 rashers bacon, 4–6 anchovy fillets, 3 tablespoons chopped parsley, thyme, marjoram, seasoning, 1 egg, fat or oil.

Make a stuffing: first sauté the onions lightly together with the bacon (or ham) chopped up into little bits. Then mix with chopped anchovy fillets (or 2 teaspoons anchovy sauce), parsley and a mixture of herbs to taste. Season with black pepper only. Bind with an egg. Increase the quantities if you would like more stuffing.

Make pockets in the round of beef with a very sharp knife. Cut into the joint in three or four places as deeply as possible without cutting right through. Put as much stuffing into each pocket as you can. Rebind the joint so that it doesn't ooze out.

Rub the surface of the meat with oil and salt. Allow 15 minutes for each lb of meat plus a further ten minutes. Roast in a hot oven, basting frequently.

Father's Other Special Roast Beef

He's full of surprises. Proceed exactly as before in the preparation of the beef. Prepare instead this stuffing to push in the little pockets.

2½–3 lb round of beef, 3 tablespoons breadcrumbs, 1 onion, 1–2 chicken livers, chopped ham (chopped tongue optional), 1 tablespoon Parmesan, 1 tablespoon liver pâté, a grated carrot, 1 tablespoon chopped parsley, mixed herbs, seasoning, 1 chopped stick celery, 1 egg.

Soak the breadcrumbs in hot water for five minutes. Squeeze dry. Mix all the ingredients together, finely chopped where necessary. Don't overherb. Bind with the egg. Insert into the pockets of your beef. Roast as instructed above. (If you can't get chicken livers, use more pâté; if no pâté, use more chicken livers.)

OR

You could buy a sizeable chunk of roasting beef which can be rolled, or unroll the joint you have bought. This latter method is a little dangerous: who knows how the butcher has prepared it, and you may never get it together again! Anyway, lay out whatever you've got and pile the stuffing on its centre. Roll and bind well with twine. Roast as above.

OR

Buy cheap stewing beef (chuck or bladebone) cut as wide as possible and fairly thin. Stuff, bind and braise in a little oil. Place in a casserole with an inch or two of water. Cover with foil and the lid. Cook in very slow oven for up to 6 hours. That's for 2 lb of very tough beef. You may need to make two or three rolls.

BEEF WITH CHILLI SAUCE

This is the one with which Father could get rid of Mother for a week or two.

1½ cups butter beans, 1 lb stewing steak, 1 onion, chilli powder, 1 tablespoon flour, oil, 3 cups stock, tomato paste, bayleaf, 2 cloves crushed garlic, 2 sprigs parsley, 1 pinch thyme, seasoning.

Soak the butter beans for an hour or two and then cook in salted water for 40 minutes plus. The cooking time will depend on the condition of the beans. They should only be cooked until they are 'al dente' (i.e. nutty).

Cut the steak into bite-size pieces. Chop the onion and sauté in oil.

Father has been warned. This effort could cause a general walk-out, so he must consider his intention carefully.

TO KEEP THE FAMILY TOGETHER: Don't use more than one level table-spoon of chilli powder. Or even less, if it is a very strong brand.

TO HAVE A LITTLE RESPITE: Double or treble the quantity of chilli powder, and for good measure, add a pinch or two of cayenne pepper. After all, it's meant to be a hot dish.

In other words use as much chilli powder as you feel like. Mix it with the flour. Dust each piece of meat in the chilli-flour mixture. Add to the onion and oil and brown. Then cover with stock and add the tomato paste, the bayleaf, the garlic, the sprigs of parsley, and the thyme. Simmer gently for a couple of hours. Season as required.

Meanwhile drain the beans if you haven't done so. Add to the meat after $1\frac{1}{2}$ hours. If they haven't been overcooked, they should absorb some of the excess liquid. If there is too much at the end, reduce by fast boiling. Serve with a salad and a vinegary vinaigrette dressing (i.e., equal parts of oil and vinegar).

Minced meat can be used instead of stewing beef. Haricot beans, soaked overnight, can be used instead of butter beans. They will require a longer cooking.

BEEF GOULASH

This is a fairly standard recipe, but Father, as usual, has one or two little tricks up his sleeve to improve it. Enough for six.

$\frac{1}{4}$ pint of beer, $1\frac{1}{2}$ lb stewing beef, 2 tablespoons flour, paprika, 1 large onion, 1 tablespoon oil, stock, 2–3 tablespoons tomato purée, seasoning, bayleaf, 1 lb potatoes, 1 cup of sour cream or a mixture of sour cream and yoghurt.

The first little trick is to open a can or bottle of beer and consume all but $\frac{1}{4}$ pint of it during cooking. Then set aside firmly. Should you lack control and drink it all, you will be forced to send out for a second can. This is likely to happen should the meat be tough and take longer to cook than expected.

Chop the steak into cubes. Dust in a mixture of flour and as much paprika as you like. Chop the onion roughly and sauté lightly in the oil. Add the meat and brown all over. A little more oil may be needed. Throw in any left-over flour and paprika as well. Cover with stock, add the tomato purée and stir well, scraping the bottom of the pan as the liquid comes to the boil. Add seasoning and a bayleaf, possibly a pinch of cayenne pepper. When the sauce has thickened slightly, place in a casserole. Cover and cook gently in the oven for $1\frac{1}{2}$–2 hours at gas mark 4. The cooking time depends on the quality of beef.

Meanwhile, half-cook the peeled potatoes. Drain and cut into sizeable chunks. When the meat is nearly cooked, add the potatoes, the cream and/or yoghurt and stir in well. Add the beer, or what's left of it. Cover the casserole and cook for a further half hour. Check seasoning before serving.

BEEF STEWS AND CASSEROLES

You can do practically anything you like with these and you've probably had something like the first recipe hundreds of times, though not necessarily with the potatoes spread on top. I've included the first one as it is simple with a pleasant vegetable taste.

Simple Casserole

1½ lb stewing beef, 1 large onion, oil, seasoning, flour, stock to cover, few pieces of celery, carrots, bayleaf, thyme, parsley, peeled sliced potatoes, nutmeg.

Chuck steak is probably best here. Cut the meat into large pieces. Chop up the onion and sauté in oil. Dust the meat in seasoned flour. Brown with the onion as it begins to soften. Tip into a casserole. Swirl a little stock around in the pan, scrape well and pour into the casserole.

Dice, slice or chop celery, carrots, herbs and any other available vegetables in moderate quantities. Add to the casserole and just cover with stock. Season. Cover and simmer in a medium oven for 1 hour.

Remove (some of the liquid should have evaporated) and spread a layer of moderately thickly sliced potatoes over the top. They should not sink down until immersed by the sauce but rest lightly on top. Season, adding a pinch of nutmeg, and brush with butter, or oil.

Raise the heat a little and cook for a further 45–60 minutes. Remove the casserole lid for the last twenty minutes of cooking to brown the surface of the potatoes.

Beef Stew or Casserole in Red Wine

I prefer to cook slowly in the oven rather than stew, but either method is acceptable.

1 onion, 2 cloves garlic, 2 rashers bacon, fat or oil, 1½ lb stewing steak, flour, seasoning, ½ cup red wine, 1 tablespoon tomato purée, bayleaf, marjoram.

Chop up the onion, the garlic, the bacon rashers, and sauté in oil. Place in a casserole. Cut up the meat into cubes, dust with flour, season and brown. Add the wine. Let it bubble and then add the tomato purée. Pour meat and sauce into the casserole. Add just enough stock or water to cover the meat, a bayleaf, and a pinch of marjoram. Mix in well. Cover the pan and cook slowly for 2–2½ hours: the time will depend on the quality of meat.

If the sauce has not evaporated enough when the meat is tender, place on top of the stove and reduce by fast boiling. The sauce should be thick and dark.

Beef Casserole and Black Olives

1½ lb stewing beef, 1 cup white wine, 2 chopped cloves garlic, parsley, bayleaf, thyme, 2 tablespoons oil, ¼ lb fat bacon, 2 carrots, 1 onion, 6–7 stoned black olives, 6 mushrooms, 3 tomatoes, seasoning, beef stock.

Cube the beef and marinade in the wine (red will do if white unavailable), garlic, a little chopped parsley, a bayleaf, a pinch thyme, and the oil. Leave for three hours. Strip the rind from the bacon and lay half in the bottom of the casserole. Cover with chopped carrot, an onion cut into rounds, chopped olives, half a dozen mushrooms, and sliced tomatoes (half a small tin Italian tomatoes would do). Sprinkle with chopped parsley, and season.

Add stock to the marinade and meat and pour the lot into the casserole over the vegetables. (Less stock if using tinned tomatoes and their juice.) Spread the remainder of the bacon over the top. The marinade and stock should just cover the meat. If you seem to have too much, don't use it all.

Put the lid on the casserole and simmer in a very slow oven for four or five hours. Seal the lid onto the base by applying a mixture of flour and water to the joins.

BEEF MOUSSAKA

You'll come across all kinds of recipes for this traditional Greek dish. It is useful for getting rid of that left-over meat that nobody seems to fancy. But it's better if freshly cooked mince is used.

1 lb minced meat, stock, $\frac{1}{2}$ cup red wine, 2 tablespoons tomato paste, 1 or 2 cloves garlic, bayleaf, mixed herbs, seasoning, 3 aubergines, 4–6 tablespoons oil, 4 onions, 3 tomatoes, 1 cup Béchamel sauce, 2 eggs, grated cheese (optional).

Cover the mince in seasoned stock. Flavour with wine, tomato paste (or purée), crushed garlic, a bayleaf, and a good pinch of mixed herbs. When cooked, most of the liquid should have evaporated. If not, reduce by fast boiling until $\frac{1}{4}$ cup is left. Cooking time is about 40 minutes over a low heat. (If using left-over meat, cooking time is much less: simply heat it through to absorb the additional flavours, and use less stock.) Season during cooking.

Slice unpeeled aubergines, salt them, and let them drain for an hour. Then fry in oil until lightly browned on both sides. Remove from pan. Slice the onions and fry in the same pan. Season. Add more oil if required. Slice some tomatoes. You can omit them, but I think it's better with.

Make 1 cup Béchamel sauce (see page 121), but use the following quantities: $1\frac{1}{2}$ tablespoons flour, $1\frac{1}{2}$ tablespoons butter, 1 cup milk, seasoning to taste and a pinch nutmeg.

Choose a smallish, deep, oven-proof casserole – or make do with a similarly deep, square or oblong buttered cake tin. Cover the bottom of the dish with a layer of aubergines. Next a layer of meat, then a layer of sliced tomatoes, and finally a layer of onion. Continue until all the ingredients are used up. Pour in the stock juices left over. However, don't let the meat and vegetables become too moist.

Beat the eggs and add them to the Béchamel sauce off the stove. Mix in well and pour over the other ingredients. Sprinkle with grated cheese. Bake in a moderate oven for 30 minutes or until the topping forms into a kind of crust and turns golden brown.

INDIVIDUAL STEAKS COOKED IN PASTRY

You will find steaks cooked in this manner highly praised. Your guests and your family will know that you have taken a lot of trouble. It is probably best to use fillet steak as it is easier to judge when it is cooked. Cooking times and oven heat should be followed carefully, otherwise you will make a mess of the pastry by poking into it with a skewer to find out if it is cooked. Time and oven temperature indicated should ensure that the meat finishes up medium-rare.

Pastry, 4 round thick steaks, seasoning, butter, 1 finely chopped onion, 8 mushrooms, 2–4 tablespoons of port, Madeira or medium-sweet sherry.

Get Mother to make the pastry or buy the frozen kind which is very good: plain or puff, although I think it is better with plain. Shape the beef into rounds and seal by dropping them into hot seasoned butter. Remove from pan. Sauté the onion and the mushrooms in the same pan. Add extra butter if necessary. Do not let the onions brown. When they and the mushrooms are soft pour in the liquor – port is definitely best. Let it bubble until it has practically evaporated. You should now have a thickish paste consisting of the mushrooms and onions flavoured by the liquor. Check the seasoning.

Meanwhile cut out some rounds of pastry, each round an inch wider in diameter than the pieces of steak. Place a piece of meat on each round. Then place the sauce on top of each. Encase each individual piece of meat and its accompaniments with the remaining pastry. You should now have produced dome-like pies with straight sides. Seal with milk or water. Make sure that none of the sauce escapes. Place on the centre shelf of a moderately hot oven for 25 minutes. This is one case when the oven *must* be pre-heated.

You can use back rib fillet mentioned on page 75: it works well and is less expensive. In this case, the cooking time should be extended to 35 minutes.

ALTERNATIVELY: you can cover a single piece of beef in pastry with the same kind of sauce. Only make more as quite a bit of it will be absorbed by the mound of pastry. Use the same oven temperature but a longer cooking time – 35 minutes. If using one of the cheaper cuts cook for 40 minutes.

BEEF IN CABBAGE LEAVES (CABBAGE DOLMAS)

This is another popular Mediterranean dish with a few additions from Father. It can be a lot of trouble to prepare but is one of the nicest ways of eating that poor, maligned cabbage.

1 small white cabbage, 2 tablespoons long grain rice, ½ lb minced beef, 2 finely chopped onions, 1 tablespoon parsley, seasoning, 1 pinch cayenne pepper, 1 small tin tomatoes, 2 grated carrots, 1½ cups stock, beurre manié.

Blanch the halved cabbage in salted water. Boil the rice and drain. Mix the rice with the mince, half of the onion, and the parsley.

Season with salt, black pepper and cayenne pepper. Separate the leaves of the cabbage, discarding the outside leaves. Place a spoonful of the meat mixture on each leaf, roll up and tie with cotton, thus forming little parcels.

Make a sauce from the tomatoes and juices, the remainder of the onion, the grated carrot and the stock, lightly thickened by using a beurre manié. Other condiments and herbs are a matter of personal taste; use what you like but proceed with reasonable caution. No more cayenne pepper however. The sauce should be well-flavoured but not fiery.(Father will use his well-known flair and imagination here.)

Place the cabbage parcels into a casserole, cover with the sauce, cover with the lid, and cook in a low oven for 1½ hours. If necessary, top up the sauce with stock. If you've hated cabbage all your life, your outlook will have changed after sampling this excellent recipe.

BEEF LOAF

You can make all kinds of meat loaf. You can use minced beef, minced veal, minced pork or a combination of all three. I think the two following ones are a little unusual.

With Corn

1 tablespoon chopped onion, 1 lb minced beef, 1 tablespoon butter or oil, 1 tablespoon flour, ½ cup milk, 1 tin corn, seasoning, 1 tablespoon chopped parsley, 1 teaspoon Worcestershire sauce, 2 tomatoes, 2 tablespoons diced bacon, 1 egg, dried breadcrumbs.

Brown the onion and the meat in the oil. Sprinkle with flour, mix; add the milk and stir well. Then add the rest of the ingredients except the raw egg and dried breadcrumbs. Allow to cool for a few minutes, then add the egg as a binding. (The can of corn should be drained and the tomatoes chopped into small pieces.)

Butter a rectangular dish and pour in the mixture. Sprinkle with the dried breadcrumbs, dot with butter, and bake in a hot oven for 45–50 minutes.

Stuffed Meat Loaf

1 lb minced beef, 1 tablespoon flour, 4 eggs, garlic, 1 onion, herbs, allspice, seasoning, 2 tablespoons grated cheese, ¼ lb ham or boiled bacon, 4–5 anchovy fillets, 2 tomatoes, 1 tablespoon chopped parsley, dry breadcrumbs.

Mix the meat with the flour, one beaten egg, a chopped clove of garlic, a chopped onion, a pinch of herbs (mixed or of your own choice) and a little of some or all of the condiments. The meat should be well spiced. Season. Place half the meat in a well-buttered rectangular tin. Press the centre down a little.

Halve the 3 remaining eggs which should have been previously hard-boiled, and mix as gently as possible with cheese, ham, chopped anchovies, and parsley. Place in the depression and cover with the remainder of the meat.

Sprinkle with breadcrumbs, brush with butter and bake in a slow oven for an hour.

HAMBURGERS

Can be served as a main meal or as a late night supper.

Spice the minced meat with nutmeg, cumin, paprika, cayenne pepper, allspice etc. Instead of serving them with a mass of greasy fried onions cover instead with:

(a)   A raisin sauce (see duck, page 105).

(b)   A chilli sauce liberally sprinkled with chopped black olives.

(c)   Pineapple chunks mixed in a sweet and sour sauce. The sauce can be made out of the juice from the tin of pineapple, vinegar, soy sauce and thickened with cornflour.

(d)   A grilled tomato placed on the top of each hamburger and covered with a thick cheese sauce, sprinkled with grated cheese and browned under the grill.

FATHER AND HIS LITTLE LAMBS

ROAST LAMB

Leg or shoulder. Spread with fat, season and roast until cooked. Cook fast or cook slow. Fast cooking is best when your joint is absolutely first class and you would like to eat it rare, as beef. But most families seem to prefer their lamb roasts well-cooked. As mentioned earlier, I came across a French recipe which suggested that a $3\frac{1}{2}$ lb leg of lamb needs only forty minutes' cooking in a hot oven. I tried it. My comment: the French certainly like their meat rare! Try a reasonable compromise. Say about $1\frac{1}{2}$ hours in a very hot oven.

Here are a couple of Father's special efforts.

Sugar Lamb Roast

1 roasting joint (leg or shoulder about 3 lb), fat, 1 teaspoon ground ginger, 2 tablespoons brown sugar, $\frac{1}{2}$ cup cider, $\frac{1}{4}$ cup stock, 1 teaspoon thyme, seasoning.

Rub the joint with fat. Sprinkle with ginger and brown sugar. Moisten with cider and stock mixed and pour the rest of the liquid into the roasting pan. Cook in a moderate oven allowing 20 minutes for each lb plus 20 minutes over, covered loosely by a piece of foil. Add the thyme and seasoning to the liquid.

Baste from time to time. You will find that the liquid will evaporate so keep adding a little more stock or cider each time you baste. If you don't do this, the sugar will caramelise and you will finish up with toffee lamb. Remove the foil for the last fifteen minutes of cooking. Use the liquid left in the pan as an excellent, sweet gravy after spooning off the surplus fat. If too thin, reduce before serving.

Roast Lamb and Garlic

Roast as usual after first inserting little slivers of garlic into cuts made in the joint. Chopped anchovies can also be used.

Roast Lamb and Orange Sauce

This is a change from the ubiquitous mint sauce.

1 joint lamb, fat, seasoning, juice of an orange, 1 teaspoon grated rind, 1 tablespoon mint, 1 teaspoon sugar.

Roast as usual. When nearly cooked, drain as much fat from the pan as you can. Pour in the orange juice together with the grated rind and the mint. Add the sugar and enough water to stop the pan juices evaporating. Baste the meat with this sauce for the remainder of the cooking time. Remove the joint. Spoon off any further fat. Add further orange juice if not orangey enough and boil until well amalgamated with the pan juices. Offer this sauce instead of mint sauce.

Roast Lamb and Madeira Sauce

Serve your joint with this magnificent sauce. It must not be brown gravy with a slurp of Madeira added. For proper preparation see page 121. If made correctly, it is superb.

Roast Lamb Stuffed with Mint

A change when fresh mint is available. Make incisions in the joint as you would for garlic, and stuff with substantial quantities of chopped mint.

Roast Lamb on a Bed of Tomatoes and Onions

1 shoulder of lamb, garlic, fat, seasoning, 1 large tin tomatoes, 3–4 sliced onions, mixed herbs, 1 lb potatoes.

Insert slivers of garlic throughout the joint. Rub with fat and seasoning. Pour the tomatoes into the roasting pan. Add the onions and sprinkle liberally with mixed herbs together with 1–2 cloves finely chopped garlic. Being a garlic maniac, as you may have gathered, I use 5–6 cloves. Place the joint on top.

Roast as usual. Baste from time to time. One hour before the joint is cooked, surround it with sliced potatoes. They should completely cover the onions and tomatoes. Sprinkle them with salt and brush with melted fat. The addition of the potatoes is optional. Before serving remove as much excess fat from the pan as you can.

Roast Lamb with Haricot or Butter Beans

As you probably can't afford to go to France for that summer holiday, you will have to prepare this popular French dish yourself.

1½ cups haricot or butter beans, 1 bayleaf, 3 cloves garlic, 1 tablespoon wine vinegar, 1 shoulder lamb, seasoning, rosemary, oil or fat, ½ cup of white wine, chopped parsley.

Soak the haricot beans overnight (or butter beans for an hour) in a marinade of salted water, a bayleaf, 2 crushed garlic cloves and vinegar. Boil the beans in the marinade, about 2 hours for the haricot beans – about 40 minutes for the butter beans. Do not overcook. They should be soft outside, nutty inside. Butter beans are easy to overcook, so watch them.

Insert slivers of garlic into the joint, season, sprinkle liberally with rosemary, and smear with oil or tiny bits of fat. Roast as usual.

Remove the cooked joint from the pan. Spoon off any fat. Add about ½ cup white wine to the remaining juices and let it bubble for a moment or two. Drain the beans. Pour the sauce over the beans and mix in a substantial amount of chopped parsley.

LAMB AND VEGETABLE PIE

1 lb lean lamb, 1 lb courgettes (cucumber or aubergines), seasoning, nutmeg, Parmesan, butter.

Slice the lamb into thin flat pieces. Slice the courgettes into circular rounds (same for the other vegetables suggested). Salt and let drain for an hour. Butter an oven dish and first place in it a layer of vegetable. Season with pepper and a dash of nutmeg. Cover with some of the meat. Sprinkle with cheese. (Grated Rat Trap will do but it's not quite as good as Parmesan for this one.) Repeat the procedure until all the ingredients have been used up. Finish with a layer of vegetable. Cover liberally with cheese and melted butter. Bake in a moderate oven. Allow an hour.

LAMB CUTLETS WITH CURRY POWDER

Lamb cutlets (best end of neck), curry powder, flour, egg, breadcrumbs, seasoning, oil.

Trim the cutlets you need. Rub a hot curry powder over each one. Dip into flour, then egg, then the breadcrumbs. Press the breadcrumbs well in. Season and fry. Serve with courgettes and tomatoes (see page 47).

SUPERIOR LEFT-OVER LAMB AND RICE

When I was a kid, Monday was a terrible night if we'd had lamb over the weekend. There was always some left. On a Monday evening we sat down to cold, fatty lamb slices, boiled potatoes and a murdered green vegetable, the lot smothered in re-heated gravy. The gravy was made out of thickened vegetable water (my mother or Mrs Beaton said it was full of goodness) and a scrap of meat juice tarted up with tomato ketchup and a dash of Worcestershire sauce. Any difference now? Anybody feel guilty? If you do, hide your shame and send Father post haste to the kitchen. He has the answer.

8 tablespoons long grain rice, 2 onions, 1½ cups chopped-up cold lamb, 1 large handful mixed dried fruit (sultanas, raisins, currants – or whatever is available), 2 cloves chopped garlic, 2 tablespoons chopped almonds or peanuts, fat, condiments of all kinds including salt and freshly ground black pepper, 1 large tin tomatoes, 4 tablespoons sour cream and/or yoghurt.

Boil the rice in salted water. Be sure that it is 'al dente'. Strain and rinse.

Put the onions, meat, dried fruit, garlic, and almonds or peanuts into a frying pan containing a good covering of melted fat. Sprinkle with lots of spicy condiments – a little of some or a lot of one or two – i.e. paprika, turmeric, cayenne pepper, mixed spice, allspice, pounded coriander, cardamom etc. – and normal seasoning. (Don't use curry powder.) Heat, mixing well together. If you haven't got a savoury mixture by now, you should have. Stir in the tomatoes and juice and the rice. Continue to cook over a gentle heat until most of the liquid has been absorbed.

Serve with an astringently dressed green salad and a sweetish chutney. Offer each gourmet sour cream and/or yoghurt. Insist that they drop a dollop smack in the middle of each delectable plateful. It makes a perfect contrast to the sweetness of the dried fruit. A filling and pleasant meal.

LAMB MOUSSAKA

See Beef Moussaka (page 81) and use left-over minced lamb instead of beef.

LAMB STEW – THE OLD-FASHIONED KIND

A stew, somehow forgotten and very filling. You'll find something like it in Mrs Beeton.

$2\frac{1}{2}$ lb scrag end of lamb (or $1\frac{1}{2}$ lb best end of neck), stock, 2–3 sticks of celery, 2 onions, $\frac{1}{2}$ lb carrots, $\frac{1}{2}$ cup pearl barley, bayleaf, mixed herbs, 1 tablespoon tomato paste, seasoning.

Braise the meat in fat. Cover with stock. Chop the celery, onions and carrots and add with the rest of the ingredients. Season. Bring to the boil and simmer for $1\frac{1}{2}$ hours. Check seasoning. Best served with a baked jacket potato. Boneless stewing lamb can be used in which case you'd need to cook for not much more than an hour.

LAMB KEBABS

A beautiful meal and simple, especially if you are going to cook it outside over charcoal. It requires little adornment. I'm sure everybody knows how to make them but I feel I must include it.

$1\frac{1}{4}$ lb lean boneless lamb, oil, marjoram, lemon juice, seasoning, onion, tomatoes, bayleaf, rice, watercress, chopped lettuce.

Cut lamb and marinade cubed pieces in oil, marjoram, lemon juice and seasoning. Then thread the meat onto skewers alternating with thick chunks of onion, halved small tomatoes, bayleaf. Grill or cook over charcoal. Lay the kebabs, still on their skewers, on bed of rice well covered with watercress or chopped lettuce.

An extra optional: add a few button mushrooms to each skewer.

LITTLE PIGGIES WHO WENT TO MARKET

ROAST PORK

This is included for those who like their crackling but can't get their crackling to crackle. If you're really nuts about it, as I am, buy the cheaper hand of pork. You'll get more fat, but you'll get more crackling.

Unless you have a good butcher, don't let him score it. Do it yourself. He'll only slap a knife across it here and there. Score the meat the night before with your sharpest knife – nice even cuts about $\frac{1}{4}''$ apart. Having done this to your satisfaction, rub the joint with a thick coating of salt. Place in the fridge. When you come to cook it the following day, see that the oven is very hot before you put it in. As hot as you can get it. Rub fat over it first and cook for at least half an hour in the hottest of ovens. Baste occasionally. When the skin begins to blister you're on your way. Turn the heat down and continue to cook the pork in a more moderate oven.

If you've forgotten to prepare the joint the night before, the following works quite well. Boil heavily salted water in your widest frying pan. Immerse every bit of the rind in it for two or three minutes. Then rub fat over it and proceed as above.

If the crackling is still not to your satisfaction towards the end of cooking, turn the heat full on for the last ten minutes.

Roast Pork without Crackling

2½ lb lean pork or a 3 lb loin of pork, seasoning, 1 teaspoon dried thyme, ½ glass white wine (or cider).

Buy your pork without rind or remove it yourself. Rub with salt and pepper and sprinkle with thyme. Place in a moderate oven with ½ cup of water and cook for 1½ hours, basting and turning the roast from time to time. Add a little more water if needed. Remove the roast and keep warm. Spoon any fat from the liquid in the bottom of the roasting dish. Add ½ glass of white wine or cider, bring to the boil for about two minutes scraping the pan as it bubbles. Serve with well-mashed potatoes.

I like this sauce so much that I increase the quantity of white wine and sprinkle with a little more thyme. If you do this, boil gently for about five minutes.

For an alternative sauce, see Pork chops with apple and plum sauce on page 89.

PORK IN CIDER

You'll find many recipes (not in this book) which call for expensive pork chops or boneless pork chops.

Unless Father wants to grill them simply, he will make do with the cheaper spare rib chops. They have very little bone which can be cut out. Make sure they're bought from a decent butcher. They can be nearly as good as the more expensive cut.

4 good-sized spare rib chops, seasoning, 1 tablespoon flour, 1 cup medium-sweet cider, stock, 2 cloves garlic, rosemary, a few capers.

Use a wide frying pan which can be covered. Otherwise, do the preliminary frying in a pan on top of the stove, transfer to a casserole and cook in the oven. Top of the stove method is better as the chops don't become too soft.

Brown the meat on both sides in the pan smeared with oil. Season as you turn the chops over. Remove. Sprinkle the flour into the remaining juices and oil. Stir to make a roux adding extra oil if necessary. Mix in the cider and up to ¼ cup of good stock. Stir until the sauce thickens. Put the meat back into the sauce together with two crushed cloves garlic and a sprig of fresh rosemary (or 1 teaspoon dried rosemary). Cover the pan and cook slowly for about thirty minutes or until the meat is tender. (Same time approximately in the oven but with a medium heat.) Spoon the sauce over the meat from time to time. Remove the rosemary before serving as you might get spiked – a muslin bag is required if using dried herbs.

Check seasoning; it should be quite peppery. Add a few capers. Chopped baby gherkins can be used instead of capers.

SWEET AND SOUR PORK

Cold pork is nice with salads, but if you're sick of salads, this might appeal.

1 chopped onion, 1 sliced green pepper, 1 grated carrot, 1 stick celery (1"-long pieces), 1 lb diced cold pork, 1 small tin pineapple cubes, ½ cup stock, 1 glass sherry, 1 tablespoon sugar, 3 tablespoons soy sauce, 4 tablespoons wine vinegar, 1 level tablespoon cornflour.

Heat a little oil in a wide frying pan and sauté the onion, green pepper, carrot, celery and diced pork. Add them in that order allowing half a minute before each addition. Keep them on a low heat, and don't let anything brown. Mix together pineapple juice from the tin, stock, sherry, sugar, soy sauce and vinegar. Tip that into the pan. Dissolve the cornflour in water. Add, and stir well before the liquids boil. When it does, the sauce should have thickened and have a translucent appearance. Season. Add the pineapple cubes and continue cooking until the meat is heated through and the vegetables are tender.

NOTE: No celery? Use another green pepper. No green pepper? Use extra celery. No green pepper? No celery? Do your best then with halved French beans. Almonds, lightly roasted under the grill, are an excellent addition.

PORK PAPRIKA

4 good-sized spare rib pork chops, 1 chopped onion, 8 sliced mushrooms, 1 tablespoon paprika, 1 pinch cayenne pepper, 1 heaped teaspoon flour, ½ cup stock, 2 tablespoons tomato paste, 4 tablespoons yoghurt, seasoning.

Remove any bone from the chops. Fry in oil for about 40 minutes or until browned and cooked through. Use a low heat. Remove and keep warm. Sauté the onion in the pan juices. When translucent, add the mushrooms. Cook for a further 3 minutes. Mix paprika, cayenne pepper and flour together. Sprinkle over the onions and mushrooms. Mix well together, then pour in the stock, squirt in the tomato paste. Season. You should now have a thickish smooth sauce. Return the chops to the pan and heat to serving temperature. When serving, any excess sauce should be spread over each chop and topped with a tablespoon of yoghurt.

PORK CHOPS WITH APPLE AND PLUM SAUCE

4 good-sized spare rib pork chops, 1 tablespoon butter, seasoning, 1 cooking apple, 3–4 stoned plums, 1 teaspoon sugar, 1 powdered clove, grated lemon rind, 1 pinch cinnamon, 1 small sherry glass of port or Madeira.

Remove bone from chops and fry in butter for 40 minutes over a low heat. Season. To make a sauce of the apple and plums, mash the fruit together with a fork. Add sugar, the powdered clove, a scraping of lemon rind, the cinnamon, and a drop or two of water. Cook over a low heat until the fruit is soft. Pour in the port or Madeira. Let it bubble for a few seconds only. Serve with the chops.

NOTE: Increase the quantities and use this sauce to accompany roast pork without crackling instead of the sauce suggested there, see page 88.

LOIN OF PORK AND ORANGE RICE

This is an unusual and decorative party dish. As it is moderately inexpensive, it can be served to the family too. Moderately inexpensive means that it will cost no more than the average week-end joint.

Breadcrumbs, 4 tablespoons butter, 1 level tablespoon basil, 1 level teaspoon thyme, 1 chopped onion, 2 teaspoons ground ginger, seasoning, 1 egg, 1 loin of pork boned from 8–10 chops, ½ cup of stoned prunes, 1–2 oranges, 1–3 tablespoons brandy.

A little self-restraint is required with the brandy bottle. You might get away with one tablespoon brandy, but three is better.

First soften the breadcrumbs by pouring boiling water over them until they swell up. Melt the butter. Then make a stuffing by mixing together the breadcrumbs, the butter, the herbs, the onion, half the ground ginger, seasoning and a beaten egg. Increase or decrease the ingredients to taste but don't make the stuffing too herby.

Having scored the meat to your satisfaction (see page 87), spread the stuffing on the inside. Embed two rows of prunes down the centre (don't use them all: reserve 6–8 for garnish), roll up the meat and secure firmly with skewers, or bind. Brush the skin with oil and sprinkle with seasoning and the remaining ginger. Bake in a moderate oven, which must have been pre-heated. Allow thirty minutes for each pound of meat plus ten minutes. You may need a drop of oil in the bottom of the pan.

While the meat cooks, immerse the rest of the prunes and at least eight segments of orange in heated brandy. Let them stand in the brandy until ready to use, then place alternate prunes and orange segments on two skewers. Lay these on top of the joint when you come to serve it.

It is essential that you accompany this meal with orange rice, see page 58.

VEAL VARIATIONS

ROAST VEAL

See note on page 21 about fillets of veal. Before you decide to roast the joint, consider your bank account, your courage and the economy of cutting out your own fillets. You'll find a sausage-shaped piece within each leg (often sold, I fear, as genuine fillet) which will provide a good piece of meat that you can cut into any thickness you like. It's worth remembering that a shoulder or leg of veal (at the time of writing) is the cheapest meat you can buy for roasting. Cash in on the prejudice against veal which no doubt is partly responsible for its relatively low cost. Roast in either of the two following ways.

Roast Veal with Lemon and Anchovy Sauce

3 tablespoons oil, juice of a lemon, 2 teaspoons anchovy sauce, freshly ground black pepper, leg or shoulder of veal.

Mix oil, lemon, anchovy sauce together. Sprinkle in a little pepper. The amounts given are for a shoulder. Increase the quantities for a leg. Spread this sauce over the joint and cook in a moderately hot oven covered loosely with a piece of foil. (The skin can get very hard; if you like a crisp crunch omit the foil.) Allow 20 minutes per lb plus 20 minutes over. Baste frequently. Don't let the sauce evaporate, so add water if necessary.

Remove the cooked joint from the pan, skim off any fat, boil and reduce, scraping the pan as you do so. Sauté potatoes will go well with this joint.

Roast Veal with Onions and Tomatoes

Garlic, leg or shoulder of veal, seasoning, oil, 3 large Spanish onions, 1 large tin tomatoes, mixed herbs.

Insert slivers of garlic into the joint. Rub with seasoning and smear with oil. Slice the onions in rings, lay in the roasting pan, and place the joint on the bed of onions. Pour a tin of tomatoes around it. Sprinkle with mixed herbs and check seasoning. Cover loosely with foil.

If the vegetables start to dry out during cooking, add a little stock. Cooking time 20 minutes per lb, plus 20 minutes over, in a moderately hot oven. When cooked, place the joint on a serving dish. Remove any excess fat from the vegetables; they should be quite moist. Serve in a separate bowl.

Most recipes would say surround the joint with vegetables, I only make a mess of the table-cloth when I carve. So I suggest you put the vegetables in a separate dish.

ESCALOPES OF VEAL

There are many variations. I have chosen four which will enhance Father's growing reputation. In all cases, the veal should be bashed as thin as possible. Cooking time: 3 minutes on each side over a gentle heat. A little longer if breadcrumbed. Recipes are, as usual, for four people.

A Simple Escalope

Bash, dip in seasoned flour, then a beaten egg, and finally breadcrumbs. Fry gently in good oil. Peel a lemon and slice it very thinly. Dip the slices into chopped parsley. Place a slice on each escalope and top with a stoned green olive. Surround the olive with little bits of chopped anchovy fillet. Mash a hard-boiled egg and sprinkle on the top. Melt a good quantity of butter until it starts to brown. Pour over the meat, garnish with parsley and serve.

Accompany with straw-like, deep-fried chips if you can be

bothered to prepare them. Otherwise ordinary chips or sauté potatoes.

Escalopes of Veal with Raisins and Sultanas

Bash, dip in seasoned flour, and cook gently in oil. Remove and keep hot. Tip out any excess oil. Pour a good $\frac{1}{4}$ cup of red wine into the pan and swish it about. Let it bubble for a minute or two. Turn heat down and add 2 tablespoons double cream, and a level teaspoon French mustard. Season very lightly. Don't let the cream boil. Add a few raisins and sultanas – or just sultanas. (These should have been plumped up previously by soaking in boiling water.) Pour the sauce over the meat.

Escalopes of Veal with Marsala and Parmesan Cheese

Bash, dip in seasoned flour, and cook gently in butter, but for not more than 1 minute on each side. Then add 2 tablespoons Marsala (or a medium-sweet sherry if all the Marsala has been drunk). Sprinkle a thick coating of Parmesan cheese on each piece of meat. Moisten with a drop of stock. Cover the pan and cook until the cheese begins to melt. Remove the escalopes for serving. There should be a little sauce in the pan. If you want more, drop a dollop of butter into the pan and further Marsala. Let it bubble gently until it goes syrupy. Spoon over the escalopes.

If you haven't any Marsala (it's quite difficult to buy) you could use a sweetish wine or sherry. It won't be the same but it is very pleasant.

Escalopes of Veal and Madeira

Bash, and cook in butter. Remove and keep hot. Make $\frac{1}{2}$ cup Béchamel sauce. Sauté about 12 button mushrooms in the same pan. Pour $\frac{1}{2}$ wine glass Madeira over them. Raise the heat to reduce the liquid. Add the Béchamel sauce, check seasoning, and add finally 2–3 tablespoons double cream. Mix well, don't let it boil, and pour over escalopes.

VEAL STEW WITH EGGS AND CREAM

This recipe is included so that you can use those bits of veal left over when you fillet the leg; or buy stewing veal.

3 tablespoons butter, 1½ lb stewing veal, 2 tablespoons chopped onion, 3 tablespoons chopped carrots, 8–12 whole button mushrooms, 2 cups stock, bayleaf, pinch of thyme, parsley, seasoning, 1 tablespoon flour, ½ lemon, 3 eggs, 2 tablespoons double cream.

Melt half the butter and sauté the meat and vegetables lightly for five minutes. Don't let the onions brown, so use a low heat. Pour in the stock, add the bayleaf, thyme, a sprig parsley, and season. Bring to the boil and simmer gently for an hour or until the meat is tender. Strain. Remove the bayleaf and what's left of the parsley sprig.

Melt the remaining butter and sprinkle with flour to make a roux. Add the strained stock and the lemon juice and stir until it thickens. Check seasoning. Allow to cool a little. Beat the eggs and mix with a little of the sauce. Return the sauce to the stove and add the eggs slowly, beating all the time until there is a further thickening. Do not allow it to boil. (It is safer to do this by placing the sauce in a saucepan which will fit into a larger saucepan containing a cup of boiling water, thus avoiding any direct heat and the distinct possibility of the eggs curdling. If you have a double saucepan, use that.) When the sauce has thickened, stir in the cream and add the meat and vegetables. Re-heat gently to serving temperature. Sprinkle with chopped parsley.

NOTE: If small pickling onions are in season, glaze them in butter by adding a little sugar until they are cooked and well browned, and omit 1 tablespoon of the chopped onion. It will improve the stew immensely.

CHAPTER 7

Father's Feathered Friends

CHICKEN

Do you always buy roasting chickens? If you do, don't in future, unless you want it for quick frying. Buy boilers instead. Don't listen to your friends! Take no notice of other cook books! Take my advice! It's something I refuse to argue about and you *can* roast them. They're better, cheaper, and tastier. They provide excellent stock and have at least laid a respectable egg or two. (A respectable egg is one laid in a nest.) In every way, they are superior to bland, battery-fed, cotton-wool-type roasting chickens. And as for those 'so-called' run arounds, I suspect that they've run no further than to the back of their cages.

The same comment applies to run-around turkeys. We live in a mass-producing age so, let's be fair, who can afford the land to let these birds have a decent scratch? It is therefore a lottery whether they're going to end up deep-frozen or sent to your local butcher, undrawn and labelled 'free range'. They've been reared under similar conditions. Is there any difference between the two, apart from cost? (Free range offerings are infinitely more expensive.) Are they worth the extra money? It's a matter of opinion, but I don't believe they are. I will continue buying deep-frozen turkeys or tough old 'flavoursome' chickens that have mothered hundreds of eggs as they have pecked themselves towards eternity.

ROASTED CHICKEN

There are all kinds of minor variations. The most common method seems to be to rub the bird with salt and butter, to stuff it with some kind of bread stuffing, and roast until cooked, sometimes overlaid with strips of streaky or fat bacon. I've made such a song and dance about using a boiler, I'd better tell you what I do.

ROASTED BOILING CHICKEN

Rub the bird with butter, sprinkle with lemon juice and seasoning, and place in a large casserole with a drop of water. Cover loosely with foil. Put the lid on the casserole and cook very slowly in the oven on a low heat. Allow $1\frac{1}{4}$ hours for each pound of drawn chicken.

About two-thirds of the way through the cooking, a lot of fatty stock will have oozed out of the bird. Pour most of this stock from the pan and return the bird to the oven. Put the stock in the fridge to cool. It will make it easier to take off the fat.

When the bird is nearly cooked remove the lid and foil, rub fresh butter over the breast and raise the heat. The skin should brown crisply. There is no need to give it any preparatory boiling.

Meanwhile take the cooled stock from the fridge and remove the fat. There will be quite a lot of it. The bird should be tenderly cooked and crisply brown. Remove from the pan.

During the final cooking, more stock will have come out of the bird, but won't be so fatty. Add this to your other stock, let the fat rise and spoon off. If necessary, reduce a little to strengthen its flavour.

You now have chicken consommé – we can't call this magnificent liquid chicken stock. Do what you like with it. Sample a little in the kitchen while you finish preparing the meal, offer it as chicken soup, or do as I do. I make a thick sauce out of it seasoned with salt and black pepper, and a pinch of nutmeg. Before serving, spoon in a little cream. There's a real chicken flavour about this sauce which you won't get from the roasters.

CHICKEN WITH ALMONDS

1 lb of cooked chicken (or turkey), 1 chopped onion, butter, 1 tablespoon flour, ¾ cup chicken stock, 2–3 tablespoons sour cream, flaked almonds, seasoning, parsley.

Chop up the cold chicken. Sauté the onion lightly in the butter. Sprinkle the flour into the pan, stir and cook gently for a further 3 minutes. Mix in the stock and finally add the cream. Stir until the sauce is smooth; it should be quite thick.

Meanwhile slightly toast the almonds under the grill. Add these and the poultry to the sauce. Season to taste. Heat through. Garnish with parsley and serve with rice.

CHICKEN WITH ASPARAGUS

4–6 pieces roasting chicken, 2 tablespoons butter, 1 tablespoon flour, 1 cup stock, 2 tablespoons double cream, seasoning, 1 tin asparagus, Parmesan.

Separate the chicken joints and fry gently in the butter. When cooked place in a gratin dish. Keep warm.

Add the flour to the pan, mix with the butter and pour in the stock slowly. When thickened, add the cream and bring back to a touch below boiling point. Season. The sauce should be quite thick, but if not thick enough, reduce by fast boiling. Drain the tin of asparagus and spread over the cooked chicken. Cover with the sauce. Sprinkle with Parmesan and brown under the grill.

CHICKEN WITH MADEIRA

4–6 pieces roasting chicken, butter, seasoning, a few mushrooms (optional), ½ cup stock, small glass Madeira, cream.

Fry the chicken pieces in butter and seasoning until cooked. Remove from the pan and keep hot. Add the stock and the Madeira to any pan juices and swish around. Reduce by fast boiling. Add a little double cream and pour over the chicken.

You can add a few sautéed mushrooms to the sauce. Garnish.

CHICKEN IN CIDER

1 smallish boiling chicken, oil, 1 onion, 2 tablespoons flour, 1 pint cider, 2 tablespoons tomato purée, herbs, seasoning.

Joint the chicken or use 4–6 chicken pieces. Dust with seasoned flour and brown in oil. Place in a casserole. Add a little more oil to pan and sauté a chopped onion until transparent. Sprinkle with 2 tablespoons flour to make an onion roux. Stir in the cider, tomato purée, a pinch of mixed herbs and season lightly. Pour over the chicken pieces and cook very slowly in a covered casserole for about 3 hours. When cooked, remove any excess fat, then stir the sauce well. Check the seasoning.

If using pieces of roasting chicken, the cooking time will be much less – about $1\frac{1}{4}$ hours.

CHICKEN IN CIDER WITH APPLES AND CREAM

This is a variation of the above recipe. Again, either kind of chicken can be used and the cooking times as above.

1 smallish boiling chicken, oil, 1 onion, 2 tablespoons flour, $\frac{1}{4}$ pint cider, 1 cup chicken stock, 2 cooking apples, 2 sticks chopped celery, seasoning.

Fry the chicken pieces as above recipe and place in a casserole, with the sautéed onion. Add the flour, make the roux and add the cider and stock. Peel and core the apples. Chop into pieces. Throw these into the sauce together with the chopped celery. Season and pour over the chicken. Cook as above recipe.

When cooked, remove the chicken, spoon off any excess fat from the sauce and reduce by fast boiling on top of the stove. Stir in the cream away from the stove. Re-heat, but do not boil. Check seasoning and pour over the chicken.

CHICKEN CASSEROLE WITH A NUT SAUCE

1 x 3–3$\frac{1}{2}$ lb roasting chicken, stock, chopped onion, chopped walnuts, flaked almonds, hazel nuts, pine nuts, seasoning, cayenne pepper, paprika, rice.

Joint the chicken, place in a casserole with a covering of stock, and cook in a medium oven until tender. Allow about $1\frac{1}{2}$ hours. Sauté the chopped onion in butter but do not brown. Pound all the nuts together and mix into the onions. You can use salted peanuts if you like but adjust the seasoning carefully, together with a pinch of cayenne pepper and paprika. Boil the rice as for fluffy rice on page 56, about a cupful for four people. When the chicken has cooked, place the strained pieces on a bed of rice. Reduce the stock by fast boiling, then add to the pounded nuts and onions. Season to taste and pour over the chicken and rice. If you want extra sauce, add more stock and it can be slightly thickened with a beurre manié.

FATHER'S SUPERIOR CHICKEN CROQUETTES

Very soft and creamy inside. Any kind of poultry can be used, and it's an excellent use of left-overs.

2 tablespoons thick Béchamel sauce, 1 finely chopped onion, 3–4 mushrooms, 2 tablespoons minced or finely chopped ham (boiled bacon will do), 1 sweetbread, 1 cup minced or finely chopped chicken, seasoning, nutmeg, egg, flour, breadcrumbs, butter.

If possible, do most of the preparations the day before. Make the thick Béchamel sauce. Sauté the onion, a few sliced mushrooms and the ham in butter until the onion is tender but not brown. Blanch the sweetbread in boiling water for $\frac{1}{2}$ minute, remove and chop as finely as possible. You may wonder about the sweetbread. You may not even like sweetbread. But not to worry: it is included for texture rather than flavour. This is what gives the croquettes that soft, creamy inside. Brains would be better, but they are very hard to get these days.

Put everything mentioned so far into a mixing bowl, together with the chicken. Season. Don't forget nutmeg, up to two good pinches. (You can add a beaten egg for binding.) Put into the fridge overnight. When you come to shape the croquettes you will find them easier to handle if the mixture is prepared in advance.

When ready to use, dip 1–2 tablespoonfuls into flour, shape, and egg and breadcrumb them.

Cook in deep fat or fry gently in a butter-oil smeared pan. Serve with a sauce of your own choice.

CHICKEN WITH CUMIN

A different taste.

1 x 3 lb roasting chicken or 4–6 chicken joints, seasoning, oil, 1 onion, 1 clove finely chopped garlic, 1 cup patna rice, 2 cups stock, 1 sliced green pepper, 3 roughly chopped tomatoes, bayleaf, diced ham or boiling bacon, ½ teaspoon ground cumin, parsley.

Joint the chicken. Sauté, seasoned, in oil. Remove from the pan and sauté the onion and garlic until soft. Don't brown. Return the chicken to the pan, cover and let it cook gently for about twenty minutes. Add a little more oil. Tip in the rice, mix it around until it takes on a transparent appearance. Pour in the stock, add the green pepper, tomatoes, a bayleaf, ham or bacon, and cumin. Bring to the boil, season, cover and simmer. When the liquid has been absorbed by the rice, it is cooked. Stir occasionally to prevent burning. Adjust seasoning during cooking. Serve garnished with chopped parsley.

GARLIC CHICKEN – WITH TWENTY CLOVES OF GARLIC

Father, this method of cooking a chicken will take all your courage. Don't be prejudiced. Don't be side-tracked. A word of warning, however: I suggest you arrange this feast for a Saturday night, especially if you have guests. Ascertain first if they intend going to church the following day. If they do, don't invite them or try another recipe. You and your family should avoid all contact with friends for twenty-four hours and move around the house at a safe distance from each other.

If by any chance you meet somebody you don't like – breathe on them.

1 x 3–4 lb chicken, 20 fat cloves garlic, butter, 1 leek, stock, seasoning.

Use a roasting chicken for this one. If the garlic doesn't put flavour into it, nothing ever will.

Peel twenty fat cloves of garlic, blanch them for a few moments in water, tip away the water and sauté the garlic in a liberal amount of butter until they are softened and golden but not brown. Remove the garlic and place in a casserole. Brown the chicken in the garlicky butter. Place the chicken on the garlic, add the thinly sliced leek and pour in enough stock to come about half-way up the 'fuming' fowl. Season.

Cook in a medium oven for about 1¼ hours. The liquor (after removing any excess fat) can be served in soup bowls, to be eaten at the same time as the chicken. Sop up this remarkable and delicious sauce with lumps of crusty bread.

CHICKEN MARYLAND

The original recipe has been badly ill-treated for far too long. Soggy old crumbed bits of chicken (even chicken dipped in batter), over-cooked fruit and doughy corn fritters. It's a meal that does involve a lot of trouble, but if you follow the recipe for corn fritters they'll be the best outside 'the good old U.S.A.'

4–6 pieces of roasting chicken, flour, 3 eggs, breadcrumbs, 4–6 firm bananas, milk, cayenne, seasoning, paprika, 1 large tin of sweet corn, butter, oil.

Prepare in three parts:

1. The Chicken

Buy joints of roasting chicken. The leg and thigh pieces are best since they can be cut into two fairly equal-sized pieces. Dry the chicken pieces before you dip in seasoned flour, then in 2 of the beaten egg yolks (reserve the whites and remaining egg for the corn fritters) and finally into dry breadcrumbs. Press the breadcrumbs well in. It is better to do the crumbing, both for the chicken and the bananas, an hour or two in advance to give the covering time to dry out and become firmer.

2. The Bananas

Cut the bananas in half, and cover with egg and breadcrumbs as above. You could use halves of peeled cored pears or halves of skinned stoned peaches instead.

3. The Corn Fritters

Mix together 2 heaped teaspoons flour, 2 tablespoons milk, a pinch of cayenne pepper, the remaining egg yolk, and 2 pinches paprika. Mix to produce a fairly thick batter. Add a large tin of drained corn (you can use an equivalent amount of frozen corn but it is more expensive). Just before cooking, fold in the 3 well-beaten egg whites.

TO COOK: Fry the bananas in butter until golden brown. You will have read in practically every cook book that onions, chicken, etc. should be fried until golden brown. Well, if the heat is too high under your bananas, they won't turn out golden brown. They'll be crunchy black, so have patience and proceed gently. This also applies to the deep frying of the chicken, which comes next.

Heat the oil until it is very hot, then turn down the heat. Slip the chicken pieces into the frying basket one by one (see note on page 19). If the first piece goes a dirty brown the fat is too hot. Let it cool a little before proceeding. (Father can eat that over-browned bit.) Each piece should only pale slightly when first immersed. Cook with the heat low for ten to twenty minutes depending on the size of the chicken pieces. They should then emerge 'golden brown'. Place in a warm oven with the bananas when cooked. Don't overcook the bananas.

If you've got another pair of hands, get them to make the fritters while the chicken cooks. Drop the corn mixture into a wide pan, well-heated and smeared with oil, 1 tablespoon at a time. Make sure they are well browned on the bottom before you attempt to turn them, otherwise they will fall apart. You'll need about seven minutes for each panful.

Serve with quartered lemon.

CHICKEN WITH CHEESE AND CREAM SAUCE

Left-over chicken is often prepared simply by immersing in a Béchamel sauce studded with button mushrooms. It's got the grand name of 'Chicken à la King' and is very pleasant. But for something a little different try this richer dish.

1½ cups cooked chicken or turkey, ½ pint Béchamel sauce, 3 tablespoons cheese, 4 tablespoons stock, 4 tablespoons double cream, seasoning, nutmeg, breadcrumbs.

Chop up the poultry. Make the Béchamel sauce. Add most of the cheese (Parmesan is best but grated cheddar will do). Stir until the cheese has melted, then add stock and double cream away from the heat. Season with pepper and a little salt, and a pinch of nutmeg. Return to the heat and warm slowly. Do not let it boil. Pour some of the sauce into a gratin dish. Put in the chicken, and cover with the remainder of the sauce. Sprinkle with breadcrumbs and a little more cheese. Place in a slow oven until the chicken is heated through – about fifteen minutes. Brown under the grill.

MEXICAN CHICKEN

Highly recommended.

4–5 good-sized chicken pieces, oil, 2 chopped onions, 1 tablespoon flour, 1 cup stock (or half and half stock and white wine), 1 red and 1 green pepper (or 2 of either colour), 2 tablespoons wine vinegar, 1 clove crushed garlic, 1 tablespoon tomato paste, 2 cloves, seasoning, 3 tablespoons sultanas, 6 stoned green olives.

Cut the chicken into convenient-sized pieces. Fry in oil until lightly browned. Remove and place in a casserole. In the same pan, fry the onion until translucent. Add oil as required. Sprinkle with flour and mix. Add the stock (and wine), stir until the sauce is smooth. Slice the peppers into thin strips. Add these to the sauce together with vinegar, garlic, tomato paste, the cloves and season to taste. Pour over the chicken pieces. They should just be covered. If not, mix in a little more stock.

When nearly cooked, add the sultanas (or mixed dried fruit) and the olives. Cooking time is variable depending on the thickness of your chicken pieces. Allow at least forty minutes in a moderate oven before adding the olives and sultanas.

Serve with boiled rice or crisp jacket potatoes.

CHICKEN WITH YOGHURT

½ cup long grain rice, 4 tablespoons butter, oil, 1 tablespoon chopped onion, 2 crushed cloves garlic, 1 x 3–3½ lb chicken (make sure you have the giblets etc.), 1½ tablespoons pine nuts or flaked almonds, 1–2 cups stock, seasoning, ½ cup sultanas, 2 tablespoons yoghurt.

Prepare the rice first by melting half the butter with the oil and sauté the onion and 1 clove crushed garlic gently. Chop the chicken liver and giblets very finely and throw these into the pan. A moment later, add the pine nuts and rice. Let the rice become translucent, then cover with stock and season. Add the sultanas. Let this mixture simmer until the rice absorbs all the stock. If it is not quite cooked when this happens, add a little more stock. The rice should finish 'al dente'.

Remove the rice mixture from the pan and stir into it the remaining butter. (Melt it first in a clean pan so that it froths but doesn't turn brown.) Stuff the chicken with some of the mixture and sew or skewer the opening carefully. Mix the second crushed clove of garlic with the yoghurt and a little seasoning. Spread half of it over the chicken. Place in a moderately hot pre-warmed oven for ten minutes. Reduce the heat to moderate and pour the remainder of the yoghurt over the bird. Baste from time to time during cooking. Allow about 1½ hours. When nearly ready, re-heat the remaining rice in the oven. Don't forget to fluff it up with a fork as it warms to a serving temperature.

The stuffing of the chicken with part of the rice is optional.

FATHER'S MIDDLE EAST MASTERPIECE

A very different taste.

Chicken pieces for four (about 3 lb cut to suit), 3 tablespoons oil, 12 stoned black olives, 4 large sliced onions, ¾ tablespoon grated lemon rind, 3 slices lemon, fat pinch cinnamon, 2 powdered cloves, 1 teaspoon ground ginger, 2 teaspoons paprika, pinch cayenne pepper, 8–10 powdered coriander seeds, seasoning, 2 roughly chopped tomatoes, 3 tablespoons butter, 2 tablespoons thin honey.

Use a casserole which can be used on top of the stove as well as in the oven. Lightly brown the chicken pieces in oil. Add the rest of the ingredients except the tomatoes, butter and honey. Season. Cover the pan and simmer until the onions begin to soften, then place the casserole in a medium oven for about forty minutes, turning the chicken from time to time so that it is well covered with the spices. Add up to ¼ cup water during cooking to ensure that the chicken doesn't dry up. Check seasoning.

Heat the tomatoes in melted butter and honey on top of the stove. When the chicken is nearly ready add to the casserole. Stir in gently. Cook for a further five minutes.

Best served with chunks of crusty French bread.

ALTERNATIVES: Cook the whole unjointed bird on top of the stove over a low heat. Carve in the kitchen and serve on the spicy onion mixture. Serve with rice instead of French bread.

CHICKEN WITH A LOT OF BLACK OLIVES

1 x 3–3½ lb chicken, 3 tablespoons oil, 1–2 cloves chopped garlic, 1½ tablespoons tomato paste, ½ cup white wine, ½ cup stock, ½ small tin tomatoes, 12 button mushrooms, 20 stoned black olives, chopped parsley.

Joint the chicken and brown in oil. Remove. Sauté the garlic gently, add the tomato paste (paste is better than the purée for this recipe) and let it start to brown. Add the wine and stock. Add the tomatoes, season, and finally add the chicken pieces. Bring to the boil and simmer gently in a covered pot for about 45 minutes. Meanwhile sauté the mushrooms whole in a little butter. Halve the black olives. Add mushrooms and olives to the chicken after 45 minutes and simmer for a further 20 minutes. Check seasoning. Sprinkle with chopped parsley before serving.

CHICKEN PIECES IN PARMESAN AND CURRY POWDER

Dust the chicken pieces in a mixture of flour, seasoning, Parmesan and curry powder (amount to suit your taste). Fry in oil or bake in the oven until brown. If the Parmesan flavour predominates, serve with a creamy chicken sauce. If more curried, serve with a curry sauce and curry accompaniments. Offer either with a green or watercress salad.

A simple curry sauce can be made by preparing a roux, adding a teaspoon of curry powder, adding seasoning and stock. It shouldn't be too thick or too hot. Not much sauce should be needed.

CHICKEN LIVERS IN MADEIRA

1¼ lb chicken livers, 1 tablespoon flour, 2 chopped onions, mushrooms, seasoning, 2 tablespoons butter, ½ cup stock, 1 wine glass Madeira.

Dust the livers in seasoned flour. Sauté the onions and a few sliced mushrooms in butter. The onions should not brown. Add the chicken livers, season, and cook slowly for 10 minutes. Remove livers, onion and mushrooms. Make a roux from the butter and flour and add the stock slowly, stirring until smooth. Cook gently for five minutes. Add the Madeira and let the sauce bubble for half a minute. Return the livers, onions and mushrooms to the pan. Immerse in the sauce until they are re-heated. Check seasoning.

Serve with rice.

CHICKEN AND RICE BUFFET

In case you missed it, see page 32.

CHICKEN STUFFING
Rice Stuffing

Two slightly different ones.

Mix together ½ cup cooked rice, 2 tablespoons seedless raisins, 1 chopped chicken liver, 1 chopped onion, 1 tablespoon chopped parsley, a few finely chopped almonds, 2 tablespoons thickened chicken stock, a pinch of nutmeg, basil and cayenne pepper, seasoning. Bind with an egg.

Apricot and Date Stuffing

Mix together 1 cup fresh breadcrumbs, 3–4 tablespoons dried apricots previously well soaked in water and cut up, about a dozen stoned dates, the juice of half a lemon, and seasoning to taste. Bind with an egg.

LAZY MAN'S CHICKEN IN RED WINE

This is Father's Coq au Vin.

4–6 pieces roasting chicken (or joint a $3\frac{1}{2}$ lb chicken yourself), flour, 3 tablespoons butter, 2 thick rashers salted pork or green bacon, 12 baby onions, 2 brimming cups red plonk, $\frac{1}{2}$ cup chicken stock, 1 chopped clove garlic, bouquet garni, seasoning, 12 button mushrooms, brandy (optional).

Dust the chicken pieces in seasoned flour and sauté in 2 tablespoons of butter until lightly browned; then put into a casserole. Cut the pork or bacon into chunky bits, peel the onions and sauté in the same pan until the onions are well browned. Then into the casserole with that lot. (If baby onions are out of season, you *could* use a large, roughly chopped onion – better to do this than go without.)

Pour the wine and stock into a saucepan. Add the garlic and bouquet garni. Season. Simmer until the liquid has been reduced by half, adding the mushrooms 5 minutes before it is ready. This is to go into the casserole, but if you intend to use the brandy, heat 1–2 tablespoons, tip it over the meat and set it alight first. When the flames die down, add the wine and mushrooms. If broke, ignore the brandy procedure and simply add the wine and mushrooms to the casserole. Cover and cook in a slow oven for about 1 hour.

When cooked, remove the chicken pieces, onions and mushrooms. Throw away the bouquet garni, and spoon off any excess fat. Make a beurre manié – 1 tablespoon butter to 1 tablespoon flour. Add it knob by knob to the liquid over a low heat until the sauce has thickened to your satisfaction. Add any seasoning you think is necessary. Pour over chicken and vegetables.

DUCK

I'm sure you'll find recipes around the house for Duck with Apples, Duck with Orange Sauce, Duck with Cherries, Duck stuffed with Sage and Onion. But have you got one for Duck with Raisins, or Sweet and Sour Duck, or Duck with Brandied Peaches?

DUCK WITH RAISIN SAUCE

1 duck, butter, seasoning, 1 lb cooking apples, 2 oranges, 2 level tablespoons seedless raisins, sugar.

Cover the duck with butter and season. Roast in a hot oven for about an hour, basting from time to time. Remove and keep hot. Spoon off the fat from the pan juices; make gravy from what is left.

Meanwhile prepare the raisin sauce. Peel, core and chop up the apples. Simmer until soft in the juice of an orange. Mash with a fork.

Add the raisins, a little sugar to taste, and mix well together. The sauce should be quite thick. Sprinkle with a little grated orange peel.

Slice a second orange and arrange on top of the duck. Add a further garnishing of sprigs of watercress. Serve with the raisin sauce and gravy.

SWEET AND SOUR DUCK

2 large onions, 4 tablespoons butter, 1 large duck, flour, 1½ cups water or chicken stock, 2 ground cloves, 2 tablespoons sugar, dried or chopped fresh mint, 2 tablespoons white vinegar, seasoning.

Chop the onions and cook gently in half the butter. When soft take out and put in a casserole. Dust the duck (try to buy a large duck as the breast on the smaller birds can be very sparse and thus uneconomical) with flour, add the rest of the butter to the pan and brown the duck. Put in the casserole. Add the stock, cloves and seasoning. Cover and cook in a moderately hot oven for 1½–2 hours, then pour nearly all the liquid from the pan. Reserve. Spread a little butter over the duck, return to the oven and cook for a further ten minutes with the heat raised to maximum. Baste. The duck should finish well browned and crisp.

When cooked, remove the duck from the pan and keep warm. Spoon off any excess fat from the pan juices, add what you have left to the previously extracted stock, place the lot in a saucepan and let it bubble to reduce while you quickly melt the sugar in 1–2 tablespoons of water until syrupy. Don't let it turn to toffee. Add it to the bubbling liquid together with the mint and vinegar until it has reduced enough to become translucent and moderately thick.

Serve sauce separately.

ROAST DUCK WITH BRANDIED PEACHES

Enough for six. Good for a dinner party.

1 cup long-grained rice, 2 tablespoons oil, 1 cup chopped celery, ½ cup chopped spring onions, 1 cup sliced mushrooms, 1 large tin peaches, 1 teaspoon mixed herbs, seasoning, 1 large duck, ½ teaspoon cinnamon, brandy.

FOR THE STUFFING: Boil the rice in salted water. Drain. While still hot, spoon in 1 tablespoon oil. Sauté the celery, onion, mushrooms in a further tablespoon oil. Do not brown. Open a tin of peaches: keep the juice. Chop up all but six halves.

Mix the onions, mushrooms, celery, chopped peach and herbs into the rice. Season lightly.

FOR THE ROASTING: Rub the duck with salt and freshly ground black pepper, and stuff with three-quarters of the prepared rice. Reserve the rest for the brandied peaches. Truss the duck and place in a baking dish. Brush all over with oil. Roast in a hot oven for the first fifteen minutes, reduce the heat to moderate, then allow a further 25 minutes for each pound. Brush with oil frequently. Cook until tender.

FOR THE PEACHES: Pour the peach juice into a saucepan with the cinnamon. Simmer for five minutes. Stir in a good $\frac{1}{4}$ cup brandy. Add the six peach halves and heat through gently. Remove the peach halves carefully. Spoon any liquid left into each portion and cover with a mound of rice.

Place the duck in the centre of a serving dish and surround with the brandied peaches.

TURKEY

ROAST CHRISTMAS TURKEY

There's glory to be had around Christmas. Most people have their own proven method of roasting a turkey. All are basically similar: with foil, without foil; loosely covered, tightly wrapped; covered with strips of fatty bacon, not covered with strips of fatty bacon.

Father is about to produce a masterpiece. The recipe is headed Christmas roast turkey because of its unique stuffing. It requires chestnuts which are difficult to get other than in the festive season. Tinned ones simply won't do. Quantities given are for a 12-lb turkey after drawing.

FOR THE ROASTING: *A turkey, dry mustard, flour, oil, lemon juice, seasoning.*

FOR THE STUFFING: *$1\frac{1}{2}$ lb chestnuts, 2 tablespoons chopped ham, $\frac{1}{2}$ lb chipolatas, 4 tablespoons butter, 2 tablespoons flour, stock, seasoning, 1 tablespoon brandy.*

Prepare the stuffing on Christmas Eve or you will be up before the lark. *First* have a little Christmas cheer with Mother; then let her get on with the tree decorations and thus fortified, you can get to work.

Nick the skin, top and bottom, of each chestnut. Plunge into boiling water. Boil for twenty minutes, then remove and skin. Be sure to remove all the inner skin which is very bitter. Try to keep the chestnuts whole. Chop up the ham into little pieces and the chipolatas into chunky pieces. Fry the chestnuts and the sausage in the butter until lightly browned. Remove from the pan and place in a deep bowl. Add two tablespoons flour to the pan juices. Cook until well amalgamated, then stir in a little stock. (This should have been prepared by boiling the turkey giblets etc. with onion, seasoning and a bouquet garni.) The sauce should be very thick. Season. When boiling, add the brandy (you'd better have a surreptitious snort yourself) and cook for not more than a minute. Pour over the chestnuts and sausage. Add the ham. Mix carefully taking care not to damage the chestnuts. Check seasoning. Let the mixture cool.

Then join Mother and have another glass of something. It is a

Christmas turkey you are preparing after all! Help her finish off the tree. Return to the kitchen and stuff the bird. Somebody will have to sew up the opening – probably Mother. All is now ready. Leave in a cool place overnight.

Or stuff the bird first thing on Christmas morning.

For a second stuffing, make one up. You can always throw it out if it is a disaster. Stuff it separately in the crop end so all is not lost. This a moment when Father can use his imagination and flair. Otherwise, use one of the conventional stuffings or the one noted at the end of this recipe.

FOR THE ROASTING: Make a paste of dry mustard, flour, oil, lemon juice, and seasoning. Quantities are up to you, but use plenty of mustard and not too much flour. As the turkey is to be cooked first on one side, then on the other, and then with the breast uppermost, divide the paste into three casually equal parts. This will ensure that the meat around the legs is properly cooked. Place the bird in the roasting pan on its side and rub the visible flesh with about a third of the paste. Turn over after about $1\frac{1}{2}$ hours and do the same to the other side. After three hours, set it upright and rub the breast with the remaining paste. A loose piece of foil should be draped over the bird until the final browning when the heat should be raised a little. Baste regularly during cooking.

You must try to calculate the exact time of cooking. Allow 15 minutes per lb for a drawn bird, plus 20 minutes extra, and cook as near to the centre of the oven as possible. (Gas Mark 5–6). Pre-heat the oven. Inform the family that lunch/dinner will be ready in 3 hours and 20 minutes. Also inform the family that if Mother has bought a stringy old cock instead of a hen, they may have to wait a little longer. After 3 hours and 20 minutes, test to see if it is cooked by wriggling the legs backwards and forwards. If they're nice and loose, everything should be all right. If not, Father will go away for a bit of Christmas cheer, and allow a further ten minutes' cooking. You can also test by sticking the bird with a skewer. If only a little liquid squirts out and it is quite clear, it is supposed to be cooked. That kind of testing has never worked for this Father although it is advocated in many cook books. The wriggling of the leg is a safer method.

This is another little refinement that you may care to try. The breast is inclined to get dry, so before inserting the stuffing, slip slivers of butter between the breast skin and the flesh. It's not as difficult as it sounds as the skin will pull away quite easily without breaking. A long finger is useful for this operation. The skin can then be pulled back into place and preferably sewn to the bird's bottom, thus sealing in butter and stuffing.

FOR THE GRAVY: Make a turkey gravy, thick or thin, from the turkey pan juices and some of the giblet stock. Remove any fat first. Or spoon off surplus fat from the pan and pour in a bottle of strong beer.

Scrape well and reduce to half its quantity. If you want to sweeten it, add a dollop of cranberry sauce or jelly.

NOTE. If cooking a turkey other than at Christmas, you are unlikely to be able to obtain chestnuts.

Try the following:

Fry a chopped onion lightly together with some chopped ham in a little butter. Remove from the pan and mix with fresh breadcrumbs, a drained tin of sweet corn, plenty of pepper and a little salt, a handful of parsley, and a few sultanas. Bind with one or two eggs depending on the size of the turkey and the quantity of stuffing you require.

Also see the second chicken stuffing on page 105 which can be used for turkey.

TURKEY CROQUETTES

See Chicken croquettes on page 99 and use the same method of preparation. This is good for left-overs.

TURKEY SLICES IN WINE

Butter a piece of foil large enough to completely enclose the turkey slices you propose to use. Make a sauce by first boiling a little red wine for a minute. Add to it several tablespoons of redcurrant jelly, a pinch of cinnamon and seasoning. Balance ingredients according to taste. Pour over the turkey slices and seal off with the overlapping foil. Heat in a slow oven for about thirty minutes.

TURKEY STROGONOFF

There's always some of the turkey left over. Cook several chopped onions in a lot of butter until soft but not browned. Dice up the last of the bird and add to the pan. Mix with the onions and heat very slowly. Stir in $3\frac{1}{2}$ tablespoons of sour cream and season. Add a drop of Worcestershire sauce. Served with boiled rice, it's very pleasant.

TURKEY PINEAPPLE LOAF

1 small tin pineapple rings, $1\frac{1}{2}$ cups cooked turkey, 2 tablespoons breadcrumbs, 6–8 sliced mushrooms, 2–3 eggs, 2 tablespoons Worcestershire sauce, 1 tablespoon tomato paste, 1 pinch cayenne pepper, 1 pinch nutmeg, seasoning, 1 tablespoon parsley, chopped almonds, $\frac{1}{2}$ cup milk.

Halve the pineapple rings and place in a buttered rectangular tin. Chop or mince the turkey very finely and mix with breadcrumbs, mushrooms, beaten eggs, the sauces and the condiments, parsley, onion and milk. Place on top of the pineapple pieces. Cook until firm – about 40 minutes in a moderate oven. Turn out onto a serving dish with the pineapple pieces uppermost. Sprinkle with chopped almonds and garnish with watercress.

CHAPTER 8

Miscellaneous Masterpieces

CABBAGE AND RING SAUSAGE

1 cabbage, salt, 1½ lb boiling ring sausage, 1 tablespoon sugar, 1 tablespoon French mustard.

Cook the cabbage as described on page 44. Heat the sausage in water. Remove and make deep incisions every inch or so but don't cut right through. Mix the sugar and French mustard. Spread over the sausage and brown under the grill – in fact, let the sugar burn a little. Serve with the crisply cooked cabbage.

FATHER'S DIFFERENT BANGERS

When I was a kid, sausages were called bangers. They still are, though heaven only knows why. You had to prick them or their skins would burst. Now you'd be lucky to get a whimper out of the wretched things. But despite this, I still love them even if you need a microscope to find the meat. To fry or grill is the usual method. Or bedded in a dish of usually soggy Yorkshire pudding. Try this.

1½ lb pork sausages, 2 cooking apples, enough beer to cover the sausages, peppercorns.

Prick (**to be** on the safe side) and grill or fry the sausages until they are lightly browned. Peel, core and slice the apples. Cover tightly and bake in a moderate oven for an hour.

If you have any stale bread around, make some breadsauce – super with sausages.

FATHER'S IDEA OF A SPANISH OMELETTE

All kinds of things can be used in this pleasantly light dish, but it is hardly worth doing with less than six eggs. Use some or all of the ingredients suggested. Father considers that lightly fried lumps of potato (large dice) should always be included.

At least six eggs, butter, cooked peas, strips of green and/or red peppers, tomatoes, diced left-over pieces of meat or poultry, chopped ham, bits of bacon, chopped onion, mushroom stalks, cooked potato, etc., seasoning.

Sauté gently in butter until tender ingredients like onion, potato, peppers, bits of bacon, meat or poultry. Tomato chunks (added last) should be no more than lightly heated. Season. Spread over the pan. Beat the eggs, season, and pour over the lightly cooked vegetables. Cook very slowly. Stir the centre of the omelette gently once or twice to allow any uncooked egg to reach the bottom of the pan. The omelette is cooked when firm. It can be a substantial meal, prepared quickly.

KIDNEYS

Four kinds: Veal, lamb, pig, and ox.

Not often served as a main meal. Generally fried and served with pieces of grilled bacon either for 'hotel' breakfast or a light lunch. I consider this a pity and offer three recipes which can be prepared for a substantial dinner. Choice of kidney will depend on personal taste and the depth of your wallet. Veal kidneys are probably the best but are difficult to buy for some reason known only to the butchers.

Lambs' kidneys are the ones most commonly used. Pigs' kidneys can be tough, but acceptable if your teeth are in good condition. Ox kidneys are strongly flavoured, but again inclined to be tough unless cooked as suggested below. They're generally used in steak and kidney mixtures.

Lamb and veal kidneys are all right fried provided they are not overcooked as they are inclined to toughen. This is a common fault, no doubt as a result of prejudice against undercooked offal. If using ox or pigs' kidneys, core them, slice them thinly and plunge them into boiling water for not more than ten seconds. Then they can be poured into a prepared sauce, or very lightly fried in butter. If you follow this method, they will remain remarkably tender.

Kidney and Mash

1–1¼ lb kidneys, butter, flour, seasoning, 4 tablespoons cream, 1 level dessertspoonful French mustard.

If using lambs' kidneys, core and slice and sauté in butter. Do not let them become crumbly. If using ox or pigs' kidneys, use the boiling water method, then place them in melted butter. Sprinkle with a little flour and season. Mix well. Add the cream and mustard. If too thick, thin with a little milk. Heat through without boiling.

Serve with mashed potatoes and a green salad.

Kidneys and Sweetcorn

1 tin sweetcorn, ¾ cup stock or milk, seasoning, 1–1¼ lb lamb kidneys, 3 tablespoons butter.

Simmer a tin of drained corn in the stock or milk. Season well, with plenty of freshly ground black pepper. When thoroughly soft, sieve.

Slice the kidneys removing the core. Sauté in two-thirds of the butter. Don't let them crumble. Remove from the pan and place on a hot dish. Re-heat the purée adding the rest of the butter. Reduce until the purée is quite thick. Check seasoning: see that it is nice and peppery. Pour over the kidneys. You'll find it a very pleasant blending of the flavours.

Kidneys and Tomatoes

1–1¼ lb kidneys, oil, 6–8 peeled button onions, ½ teaspoon sugar, 1 chopped rasher bacon, mushrooms, 1 small glass port or cider (a little more if using cider), 1 large tin tomatoes, marjoram, seasoning.

Core and slice the kidneys. Sauté in oil until tender (or use the boiling water method). Remove. Sauté the onions in the pan juice. Sprinkle each one with a little sugar. When browned and glazed, remove. Sauté the chopped bacon and a few sliced mushrooms for one or two minutes. Next, pour the liquor into the pan and when it bubbles add the tin of tomatoes, a pinch of marjoram and seasoning. Simmer on a medium heat until the liquid is reduced by half. Return the onions and the kidneys to the pan. Simmer on a low heat until everything is well amalgamated and hot. Serve garnished.

LIVER

There are four main kinds of liver that you might be able to buy. Calf's, lamb, pig and ox. Calf's liver is considered best by many, lamb's liver (well soaked in milk) almost as tender and useful because it cooks very quickly; pig and ox are cheaper but tougher and rougher. Mind you, calf's liver is almost unprocurable at the moment, and you may get a stiff note from your bank manager if you're lucky enough to find any.

Liver with Madeira Sauce

As you know, liver is mainly fried and covered with a gravy made from the pan scrapings. Well, sooner or later, Father is going to have to buy a bottle of Madeira, so why not now and have a go at the following recipe. Although the wine is expensive, it is comparatively inexpensive to use, will enhance many recipes and should last quite a long time unless someone is in the habit of sneaking a glass or two to have with a chunk of fruit cake. The danger period is around Christmas.

$1\frac{1}{4}$ lb sliced lamb's liver, chives and parsley, butter, seasoning, flour, $\frac{1}{2}$ cup stock, 1 wine glass Madeira.

Having soaked the liver in milk for about an hour, pour boiling water over it, strain, dry, and dust with seasoned flour. Chop a handful of parsley and a few fresh chives. (If no fresh chives, use the green of a spring onion or a little minutely chopped onion.) Sauté the chives and parsley in a good dollop of butter. Add the liver, season and cook. Do not overcook as it tends to become tough – about five minutes on each side at most. Remove the liver slices to a hot serving dish. Sprinkle a little flour into the pan juices and scrape the pan well. Then add the stock and the Madeira. Cook on a low heat until the sauce is well amalgamated. Pour over the liver and garnish.

Liver Strogonoff

$\frac{3}{4}$ lb sliced lamb's liver (pig's will do), butter, 1 onion, mushrooms, flour, $\frac{1}{2}$ cup stock (or stock and white wine), 1 carton sour cream, seasoning.

Pour boiling water over the liver. Strain, dry, dust with seasoned flour and cook gently in melted butter for not more than ten minutes. Remove from the pan and keep warm. Sauté a chopped onion in the pan juices, adding a little more butter if necessary to ensure they don't brown, and finally several sliced mushrooms. When cooked, sprinkle with flour and mix together. Add the stock (or stock and white wine) slowly, and stir until the sauce is smooth. Return the liver to the pan. Pour in the sour cream and heat until it bubbles. If too thick, thin with a little milk. Season to taste.
Serve with rice and a watercress salad.

MUSTARD RABBIT

Once so popular, once so cheap, rabbit is now sadly disappearing from the average household menu. Don't roast it – it's inclined to be dry. Don't cook the tame one – it'll upset the kids.

1 rabbit, 4 tablespoons French mustard, 1 tablespoon flour, butter, 1 slice salt or belly of pork (or failing that 2 rashers of lean bacon), 1 onion, 1 chopped clove garlic, $\frac{1}{2}$ cup stock, $\frac{1}{2}$ cup cream, tarragon, seasoning, croûtons.

Joint the rabbit and smear fairly thickly with French mustard. Let it stand for an hour or two, then dip into seasoned flour. Brown the pieces in fat. Place them in a casserole. Chop the pork into small pieces and brown lightly with the onion and garlic. Add to the casserole together with any pan juices. Pour in the stock and the cream, sprinkle with tarragon, and season. Mix well. Cover with foil and then the lid of the casserole. Cook in a slow oven for $1\frac{1}{2}$–2 hours. Stir occasionally and add a little more stock if the liquid is evaporating. Check seasoning when cooked. Scatter a few croûtons over the completed dish.

A croûton (if you don't know) is a piece of diced bread fried in a lot of fat until crisp and golden. If preferred, thicken the sauce with a beurre manié.

SOUFFLÉS

The making of a good soufflé appears a mystery to many. It's simple to make if the procedure is followed carefully. It's a much praised dish. Make a good one and your guest will sing the 'Hallelujah Chorus'. It is advisable to see that everybody is seated at the table so that the soufflé can be taken straight from the oven and served. It's cooked when it is nicely brown on top and quite firm.

A Basic Recipe for Cheese Soufflé

4 tablespoons butter, $\frac{1}{2}$ cup flour, 2 cups milk, salt, 4 eggs, 4 tablespoons grated cheese.

Melt the butter and add the flour. Mix, but don't let the roux brown. Add the milk, little by little until you have a creamy sauce. Add salt. Cook for 5–7 minutes, then remove from the stove and allow to cool. Beat the yolks of the eggs and mix in. Then add the cheese reserving some for topping. Whip the whites of the eggs stiffly and fold in. Pour into a buttered gratin dish, sprinkle with cheese and bake in a hot oven (pre-heated) for 20–25 minutes.

VARIATIONS: To make it go further, spread a layer of well-mashed potatoes in the bottom of the buttered gratin dish. Then cover with a layer of one of the following:

1. A drained tin of tuna.
2. A drained tin of salmon.
3. A mixture of left-over chopped chicken and sautéed mushrooms.
4. Diced cold meat of almost any sort mixed with grated cheese.
5. Cooked vegetables, e.g. finely chopped spinach, mashed cauliflower,
6. sautéed rounds of courgettes etc.

Pour a plain soufflé mixture over the top, sprinkle with cheese and cook as above.

Alternatively you can omit the potato and mix your chosen ingredient into the plain soufflé mixture after adding the beaten eggs. This is another one where Father can let his imagination run riot.

SPAGHETTI WITH MUSSELS

Spaghetti with a meat sauce and lashings of Parmesan cheese is all too familiar. What about spaghetti and mussels?

Spaghetti for four, 4–5 pints mussels, 1 chopped onion, 1–3 cloves garlic, 1 tablespoon oil, 1 large tin tomatoes, seasoning, parsley.

Measure the waistlines of family and guests, and cook an appropriate amount of spaghetti in salted water until 'al dente'. Strain and keep hot.

Beard and clean the mussels thoroughly. Put in a pot with about $\frac{1}{4}$ cup water. Turn the heat up. When the shells open remove the mussels, strain and keep the liquid. (See Moules à la marinière page 66 for details about cooking mussels.) Sauté the onions and garlic in the oil. This is a dish which, in my opinion, is better with an extravagant use of garlic. Pour the tomatoes and juice into the pan. Season. Add the mussel stock to the onions and tomatoes to enrich their flavour. Turn up the heat. When the liquid has reduced by half (or even more) tip in the mussels but re-heat gently. Adjust seasoning. Pour over the cooked spaghetti. Don't spoil it with cheese; just sprinkle with parsley.

A Few Sauces and Dressings

BÉCHAMEL SAUCE THAT NEVER GOES LUMPY

A versatile and much used sauce and uses 1 cupful (i.e. $\frac{1}{2}$ pt) of milk. Make a roux of 2 tablespoons butter and 2 tablespoons flour. Don't let it brown. Add a little milk and wait until it boils. Then stir briskly. When the milk is well stirred into the roux, add a little more milk, up to a total of not more than half a cup. Wait until it boils. Do *not* attempt to stir until this happens. Then stir as hard as you can. Add the rest of the milk and carry out the same procedure. Season to taste, always add a little nutmeg. You should now have 1 cupful of perfectly smooth sauce. If you want a thinner sauce, more milk can now be added safely and stirred in. To get rid of any uncooked flour taste the total cooking time should not be less than 6–7 minutes.

CHEESE SAUCE (MORNAY SAUCE)

Make a Béchamel sauce as above and let it reduce a third by fast boiling. Add 2 tablespoons grated cheese and continue to stir until it is melted. Remove from the heat and add a spoonful of cream.

SAUCE MADÈRE

Quite superb if properly made – made badly so often out of a bit of old gravy tarted up with a drop of Madeira. Father would never commit such a crime. Instead he will:

Sauté a finely chopped onion and carrot in a little butter, then add 1 tablespoon of tomato purée, a spoonful of meat glaze if there is any available, 1 cup of stock, a bayleaf, thyme and parsley. Simmer for thirty minutes. Strain, return to the stove and re-heat. Thicken slightly with a beurre manié. When bubbling, turn the heat off and stir in a sherry glass of Madeira. Do not cook the Madeira as you would with most other wines.

Before serving, melt 4 tablespoons butter in a separate pan until it has a touch of brown in it. Pour into the sauce just before serving.

TOMATO SAUCE (not to be confused with tomato ketchup)

1. I only attempt this method when there is a glut of tomatoes. If you've got a deep freeze and the tomatoes are cheap, make extra. The sauce freezes well.

   Chop roughly, two pounds tomatoes, 1 stick celery, a few sprigs parsley, a carrot and an onion. Put in a saucepan with a level teaspoon sugar and a bayleaf. Add a little stock. Simmer, covered, until the tomatoes and the vegetables are a nice mush. Sieve. Season when using.

2. I'm an admirer of Italian tinned tomatoes. They are full of flavour if inclined to be a little tart, are convenient, and cheap. A little sugar and a longer cooking will reduce the tartness. Pour a tin of tomatoes into a saucepan, add a pinch of sugar and heat. Mash the tomatoes with a fork as the liquid simmers. Most people will sieve the sauce, I don't. I like the pulpy bits. Season when using.

3. Thin a tin of tomato purée with a little good stock. Acceptable when you're in a hurry.

HAM SAUCE

This is worth doing if you have some really good chicken stock. Slice $\frac{1}{2}$ cup ham into thin strips and sauté very gently in butter. Add a good squirt of tomato paste. Let it start to darken, then pour in $1\frac{1}{2}$–2 cups stock. Reduce by half. Goes with rice and Parmesan cheese.

VINAIGRETTE

Basically 3 parts oil to 1 part wine vinegar. Some would say 2 parts to 1: any further additions are a matter of personal taste – i.e. finely chopped onion, finely chopped or crushed garlic, parsley, chives, tarragon, capers, seasoning, dry mustard, even mashed hard-boiled eggs. It's up to Father.

SAUCE TARTARE

This is mayonnaise with very finely chopped tarragon, capers, parsley, gherkin, spring onion. Better to mince the additions rather than to chop.

MUSHROOM SAUCE

Fry in butter and oil, a chopped onion, chopped parsley and a crushed clove of garlic. Sprinkle with flour. Add 1–2 cups sliced mushrooms and $\frac{1}{4}$ cup water. Season and simmer until mushrooms are cooked. You'll get quite a lot of liquid out of the mushrooms. If not enough, add more water but don't let the mixture get too thin. Drop some butter into it before serving. Excellent with steak and chicken.

CLASSIC MAYONNAISE

Beat the yolks of two eggs in a soup plate. Season with a pinch of salt and the same of black pepper. Beat with a fork as 1 cup of oil is added. Start very slowly, a drop at a time, then increase the flow to a trickle until all the oil has been incorporated in the sauce. Don't stop beating for a second. Finally, add a tablespoon of wine vinegar, or if preferred, lemon juice.

That's the way most people do it if they haven't bought a bottle of the stuff already prepared. Father's method is simpler, if rather expensive. Mindful of the strain on his muscles, he will buy a liquidizer . . . He'll break the eggs into it, whites and all (unless he's going to attempt to make meringues later) and add the seasoning, vinegar and oil in one impetuous flurry of activity. Then he'll turn the machine on and in thirty seconds he'll have a mayonnaise thick, shiny, and smooth.

SWEET-SOUR SAUCE

The basic sauce is made by melting 1 tablespoon sugar in $\frac{1}{4}$ cup of warm water. To this add 1 tablespoon wine vinegar. Boil gently. You can balance this to your own taste – more vinegar and less sugar, or vice versa. It can be thickened a little by adding $\frac{1}{2}$ teaspoon cornflour mixed with water into a smooth, running paste.

Improved by throwing in a handful of fresh chopped mint. Other additions are sultanas, pine nuts, grated carrot, redcurrant jelly, chopped flaked almonds, even grated dark chocolate. Tinned syrupy fruit juice such as pineapple is interesting if used with or instead of sugar: chuck in the cubes of pineapple as well.

DAD'S SALAD DRESSING – THICK

Mix $\frac{1}{2}$ cup cream cheese with a little blue cheese, 1 minced onion, and a slurp of Worcestershire sauce. Season.

CHAPTER 10

Midnight Feasts or TV Titbits

Lovely, when the family is snoring. Private, satisfying snacks.

OR

Ideal when your wife is hungry, you are hungry, or the kids didn't get enough for dinner.

OR

The TV programmes are boring and you know the commercials off by heart.

OR

Your guests are so stimulated by your witty conversation that they won't go home.

SANDWICHES

You can do a quite a lot with two pieces of bread (brown bread is best). You'll be familiar with some of the suggestions noted below, but they are included in case they're forgotten. They can be stored in a deep freeze for 2–3 weeks if sealed in moisture-proof bags and thawed out in a couple of hours. (Avoid egg, and predominantly salad type sandwiches; they don't freeze well.)

(a)   Grated carrot mixed with chopped nuts and parsley moistened with mayonnaise.

(b)   Chopped salami mixed with mashed hard-boiled eggs and lemon juice.

(c)   Cream cheese mixed with crisp bits of bacon and shredded lettuce. Spread on bread and cover with very thin slices of tomato. Season.

(d)   Cream cheese mixed with sweetcorn.

(e)   Use a tin of tuna. Pour off the oil, flake and mix with finely chopped capers or gherkins.

(f)   Mix a drained tin of salmon with chopped cucumber and a squirt of lemon.

(g)   Sliced mushrooms, cooked or raw, blended with finely chopped chicken, grated cheese, grated cucumber and a dollop of mayonnaise.

(h)   Finely chopped left-over meat mixed with a dash of curry powder, a spoonful of chutney, grated carrot, grated apple and a few chopped nuts.

(i)   If you've got a few left-over prawns, then chop them up and mix with chopped green pepper, a drop of mayonnaise, a touch of cayenne pepper, shredded cucumber and shredded lettuce.

(j)   Mash a banana and mix with honey, lemon juice, chopped up dates and nuts.

TOASTED SANDWICHES

Toast two thin slices of bread on one side only (you will have to use the grill for this instead of the electric toaster), place the filling on the toasted side, cover with the second slice, the untoasted side uppermost. Place under the grill, brown, and then turn the sandwich over and repeat. Or, if you prefer, make an ordinary sandwich and toast it on top and bottom.

If you want the centre of your sandwich really warm, place the filling on the bottom piece of bread and push it under the grill for a few minutes before covering with the top layer. Use a little butter on the insides of the bread, but not too much.

(a)   Cover the lower slice with butter and thin pieces of cheese. Place under the grill until the cheese starts to soften. Remove and cover with sliced or mashed bananas, and finally the top piece of bread. Toast on both sides.

(b)   Mash sardines with chopped parsley and lemon juice. Top this mixture with thinly sliced seasoned tomatoes. Give it a moment under the grill, then complete the sandwich and toast on both sides.

(c)   Mix flaked tuna fish with grated cheese and butter. Top with thin slices of lightly salted cucumber. Close the sandwich and toast on both sides.

(d)   This time use two thinly sliced pieces of bread toasted on both sides. Butter one slice, cover with thin slivers of tomato and sprinkle with finely chopped bits of onion and chutney. Close the sandwich. Crown the lot with a thin slice of cheese so that the toast is completely covered. Brown this mound under the grill.

(e)   And this time, a fried cheese sandwich. Grate some cheese, season well with dry mustard and mix with a beaten egg. Spread this paste over a slice of bread and cover with another slice. Trim off the crusts, cut into four and fry both sides in oil.

(f)   Some of the fillings suggested for ordinary sandwiches can be prepared as toasted sandwiches.

SERVED ON BUTTERED TOAST

We all know about scrambled, fried or poached eggs on toast. Here's something you mightn't think of.

(a)   Grilled gammon topped with a ring of pineapple.

(b)   Hard-boiled eggs, halved or quartered and mixed into a curried Béchamel sauce.

(c)   Scraps of chicken and/or ham mixed into a thick Béchamel sauce. Pour over the buttered toast, sprinkle with Parmesan or finely grated cheese and brown under the grill.

(d)   A tin of tuna or salmon, drained, and mixed into a thick Béchamel sauce.

(e)   Make a mixture of chopped hard-boiled eggs, bits of crisp bacon, chopped parsley and a little very thick, strongly flavoured chicken soup. (You could also use bits of chopped chicken or cubes of lean cooked pork – omit the hard-boiled eggs if you want to. It's a question of how much meat you have left over and how many gaping mouths you have to feed.)

(f) Butter a piece of toast, cover with slices of tomato, sprinkle with grated cheese and place under the grill until the cheese is soft. Pop a fried or poached egg on the top.

(g) Simmer some sliced kidneys in stock and a little port. Thicken the sauce slightly with a beurre manié and pour over the toast.

(h) Mash some drained sardines with finely chopped hard-boiled eggs, mayonnaise, lemon juice, curry powder, and a dash of seasoning (very little). Spread on the buttered toast. You can warm this mixture slightly in the oven if it is still hot or very gently under the grill.

(i) Melt grated cheese in a little beer. Season with cayenne pepper, allow to cool and beat in the yolk of an egg. Peel, core and slice an apple into rings. Sauté gently in butter. Place the rings on a piece of lightly buttered toast, cover with cheese and brown under the grill.

EGG SNACKS

Eggs were called 'googies' where I came from when I was a kid. My more literate friends referred to them as hen fruit. Whatever they're called nowadays, very few of us tire of them and they are about the cheapest way of supplying protein in the diet. Father will endeavour to turn out something other than boiled, fried or poached googies. The following should please.

EGG AND TOMATO IN RAMEKINS

2 tomatoes, oil, seasoning, breadcrumbs, parsley, 4 eggs.

You will need four individual oven-proof ramekins for this.

Cut the tomatoes in half. Heat the oil in a frying pan and place the tomatoes in it with the cut side face down. Cook them slowly for a few minutes. Turn them over and do the same on the other side. Don't overcook. Remove from the pan while still firm and place one half in each dish. Season. Sprinkle with a few breadcrumbs and chopped parsley. Break an egg over each tomato half. Season again lightly. Place in the oven until the whites are firm.

Can also be served as an hors d'oeuvre.

EGGS AND A FEW PRAWNS

6 eggs, 6 prawns, butter, ½ cup cream, 1 level dessertspoon French mustard, chopped parsley, chopped chervil, breadcrumbs, seasoning, grated cheese.

Hard-boil the eggs. Shell and shred them. Chop up the prawns. Melt 1 tablespoon butter. Mix together with the remaining ingredients except the cheese. Place in an oven-proof dish and sprinkle liberally with grated cheese. Dot with butter and bake in a hot oven until the cheese begins to melt.

Serve with watercress.

EGG AND MASHED POTATO

This is a hungry man's snack. No quantities given. Mash some potatoes with melted butter and hot milk. Season with salt, pepper and nutmeg. Half-fill an *oven-proof* soup plate with potato. Make an indent in the centre. Break an egg into it carefully. Cover with a previously prepared thick Béchamel sauce. Sprinkle with cheese. Bake in a hot oven for 5 minutes. The cheese should have started to melt, and the egg should still be runny under its coating of sauce. Very tasty when you come to eat it and the yolk should run into the potatoes, so be sure that you don't cook it for too long. If very hungry, use two eggs.

OMELETTES

All kinds. A lot of nonsense is talked about how to cook them! Always use the same pan; it must be copper and never washed; it should be washed; it doesn't have to be copper; fold over gently; stir; don't stir; slide out; beat the eggs; don't beat the eggs; should be runny; should be dry and firm; etc. etc.

Therefore use your own method. This note is included just to remind Father of some of the many different fillings for omelettes: cheese, herbs, tomato, onion, chicken and ham, mushroom, bacon or salt pork (watch seasoning), potato, mussel, tuna fish.

The main thing is not to beat the eggs too savagely. Don't put in too much filling. The eggs are the main thing. Some of the fillings should be gently sautéed in butter until soft before dropping into the centre of your partly cooked omelette and preparatory to turning out onto a plate.

CHEESE SNACKS

BANANAS, HAM AND CHEESE

If you're as mad as I am, you'll have a go at this. Spread mixed English mustard over whole bananas. (You can use French mustard.) Wrap each banana in a slice of ham. Make a thick cheese sauce, see page 121. Place the bananas and ham in heat-proof dish. Pour the cheese sauce over them. Sprinkle with grated cheese and bake in a moderate oven for 10 minutes, then brown under the grill. Don't let the bananas get too soft. They might not need ten minutes in the oven if very ripe.

HOT CHEESE AND FRENCH BREAD

Slice a French loaf into pieces less than $\frac{1}{2}$ inch thick. On each piece of bread, place a thick slice of Bel Paese, Gruyère or Mozzarella cheese (if you can get it). Arrange in an oven dish so that each piece of bread and cheese overlaps. Place in a hot oven until the cheese begins to melt. Don't let it run all over the place. Chop up half a dozen anchovy fillets and heat them in 4 tablespoons of butter. Pour over the bread and cheese before serving.

BLUE CHEESE AND BRANDY OR PORT

Roquefort cheese is best but expensive. Use the cheaper Danish blue, it's very pleasant. Mix $\frac{1}{4}$ lb cheese with 3 tablespoons unsalted butter. Season with freshly ground black pepper and beat in 1 tablespoon heated brandy or port. Let it stand for at least an hour and chill slightly. Serve with crusty French bread.

SOFT ROE SNACK

A quantity of fresh roes as required. You can use tinned roes but drain them first. Lay in a small buttered oven dish. Squirt in a little lemon juice and a little grated peel. Cover with sliced tomatoes and chopped parsley. Pour in several tablespoons white wine. Season. Cover with breadcrumbs, dot with butter and heat gently in the oven for 10–15 minutes, then brown lightly under the grill.

CHAPTER 11

Sugar Daddy

BANANAS AND RUM

Peel and split four bananas lengthwise and coat with icing sugar. Place in a small fire-proof dish. Sprinkle with fresh orange juice, sugar, a pinch of cinnamon and a teaspoon of rum.

Place under the grill until the bananas are brown and have started to soften. Pour a further two tablespoons of rum over them and set it alight.

MELON SURPRISE

Don't attempt this recipe unless you can get fresh fruit. You could *just* get away with tinned cherries if you don't use the syrup.

Cut the lid off a large good melon. Remove the seeds, then scoop out most of the flesh. Cut this into dice. Mix with strawberries, raspberries, stoned cherries, and a chopped banana. Sprinkle with icing sugar. When the icing sugar dissolves and is well mixed in, place the fruit back into the melon shell. Pour in a wine glass of semi-sweet white wine and chill for at least an hour.

Quantities of fruit will depend on the size of the melon. Equal quantities of strawberries and raspberries, one banana is enough even for a large melon, and as many cherries as you like.

PEARS IN WINE

Peel and core four cooking apples. Cook in a little water, a pinch of cinnamon and sugar to taste. Mash into a purée. Peel and core four pears. Halve them. Boil 1 cup red wine together with $\frac{1}{2}$ cup sugar and a little grated lemon until it starts to go syrupy. Add the pears and cook very gently. Don't overcook them so they disintegrate. Let everything get cold.

Place the apple purée into a serving dish, arrange the pear halves on top, add $\frac{1}{4}$ cup chopped walnuts to the syrup and pour over the pears.

FRESH PEACHES

Drop the peach you are eating into the wine you are drinking. Continue to drink and continue to eat. The simplest recipe in the book.

CREAM AND WHISKY DELIGHT

Whip $\frac{1}{2}$ large carton of double cream until stiff, but avoid making it into butter. Stir in $\frac{1}{4}$ pint whisky and 3 tablespoons of thin honey. Serve in individual glasses. Drop one or two ratafia biscuits on the top of each serving. Offer extra for those who like them.

ICE CREAM SURPRISE

Use bananas or seedless grapes. Put them in a heat-proof dish, cover completely with ice-cream, then with a thick coating of brown sugar. Place under a very hot grill until the sugar begins to bubble.

OGEN MELON

Halve and scoop out the pips. Then some of the flesh. Cut this into dice and mix gently with cream cheese and a quantity of honey to taste. Put back in the melon and chill.

ORANGE SOUFFLÉ

If you've managed to make an ordinary soufflé and you feel ambitious, then:

3 tablespoons butter, $\frac{1}{4}$ cup sugar, $\frac{1}{3}$ cup flour, 1 cup milk, 1 orange, 4 eggs, 1 glass Curaçao.

Cream the butter and sugar and add the flour. Mix well. Place on a low heat and add the milk gradually. Give it a good whisk so that it becomes nice and creamy. Let it cool. Grate a little orange peel, then squeeze the orange. Beat the egg yolks and pour into the prepared mixture. Add the liquor, and the orange grating. Then add the orange juice, little by little – you may not need it all – so that you have the right consistency. Don't let it get too wet. Whip the whites stiffly and fold in. Butter a gratin dish or one with straightish sides (a circular one would be best) and pour in the preparation. Don't fill it right up or you'll have soufflé all over the bottom of the stove. Cook in a moderate oven for 20 minutes.

The more you whip during preparation the better your soufflé will be.

BAKED APPLES WITH RUM AND OTHER THINGS

Core large apples. Make an incision with a sharp knife around their middles. Place in a baking dish so that they don't touch each other. Make a mixture of sultanas, a little cinnamon, a drop or two of thin honey (or a teaspoon brown sugar) and a drop or two of rum. Put this mixture where the cores were. Add a little water and rum to the pan. Bake in a moderate oven until they become fluffy around the centre.

Serve with whipped cream.

HONEY ORANGES

Peel 6–8 good oranges and separate the segments. Arrange in a cartwheel on a circular serving plate. Mix the juice of half lemon, 1 teaspoon ground cinnamon, 3 tablespoons honey, and heat gently until the liquid comes to the boil. Add 1 tablespoon whisky. Continue cooking for a further 10 seconds. Pour over the oranges while still hot. Chill. Simple and refreshing.

CHAPTER 12

Father's Drunken Drinks

A SIMPLE PUNCH

Melt 1 cup of sugar in a little water until it turns to syrup. Add the juice of six lemons. Pour a small tin of crushed pineapple and its juices into a large bowl, add the hot syrup, and ½ bottle of rum. Chill. When ice cold, add the juice of three or four oranges and a bottle of cold champagne.

RUM PUNCH

Pour the juice of two oranges and two lemons, a bottle of rum, a tin of pineapple pieces and its juice, and four tablespoons Grand Marnier into a large bowl. Add a small bottle of Maraschino cherries and its juice. Slice an orange and lemon thinly. De-pip the pieces and throw those in too. Let the punch stand for about three hours. When ready to use, pour in crushed ice, sugar and soda water to taste.

RUM AND PERNOD COCKTAIL

Enough for one. Mix and shake together the juice of ½ lemon, two tablespoons white rum, a drop of Pernod, sugar to taste, and crushed ice.

PORT AND CLARET MULL

Pour two bottles of cheap claret and one of ruby port into a saucepan. Add 12 cloves, a cup of brown sugar, the rind of two lemons and a teaspoon of cinnamon. Heat the wine very, very slowly otherwise you will lose the alcohol content. It should take at least an hour to get to drinking temperature.

A SWEET PUNCH

Melt 1 cup sugar in 4 cups weak tea. Stir until the sugar has dissolved. Add 1½ cups rum, 2 cloves, the juice of an orange and lemon together with a little grated lemon. Heat, but do not allow to boil. Serve hot or cold.

A LETHAL DRINK

Lace very cold champagne with brandy. Whoops!

A TUMMY WARMER

Heat the following together until nearly boiling: ½ dozen drops Curaçao, 1 teaspoon sugar and 1 glass port. Sprinkle with nutmeg and serve hot with a slice of lemon.

BLACK VELVET

Another drink with a mighty kick. Fifty-fifty Guinness with dry champagne. Some of your friends will say that it is the ruination of the champagne; others, that it is a dreadful thing to do to Guinness. Use a cheap champagne, or even a good sparkling dry white wine. The slightly cloying quality of the stout blends well with the acidity of the wine, which should be well-chilled before adding the Guinness.

INDEX